THE THIRD DEGREE

The Third Degree

The Triple Murder That Shook Washington and
Changed American Criminal Justice

SCOTT D. SELIGMAN

Potomac Books

AN IMPRINT OF THE UNIVERSITY OF NEBRASKA PRESS

Library of Congress Cataloging-in-Publication Data
Names: Seligman, Scott D.
Title: The third degree: the triple murder that shook
Washington and changed American criminal justice.
Description: Lincoln [Nebraska]:
Potomac Books, an imprint of the
University of Nebraska Press, 2018.
Includes bibliographical references and index.
Identifiers: LCCN 2017044663
ISBN 9781612349947 (cloth: alk. paper)
ISBN 9781640120600 (epub)
ISBN 9781640120617 (mobi)
ISBN 9781640120624 (pdf)
Subjects: LCSH: Wan, Ziang Sung—Trials, litigation, etc.
| Trials (Murder)—United States. | Diplomats—China. |
Diplomats—Crimes against—United States.
Classification: LCC KF224.W29 S43 2018 |
DDC 345.73/062—dc23 LC record available at
https://lccn.loc.gov/2017044663

Set in Minion Pro by Mikala R Kolander

In police and criminal procedure and practice, the officer of the law administers the "first degree," so called, when he makes the arrest. When taken to the place of confinement, there is the "second degree." When the prisoner is taken into private quarters and there interrogated as to his goings and comings, or asked to explain what he may be doing with Mr. Brown's broken and dismantled jewelry in his possession, to take off a rubber-heeled shoe he may be wearing in order to compare it with a footprint in a burglarized premises, or even to explain the blood stains on his hands and clothing, that, hypothetically, illustrates what would be called the "third degree."

—Major RICHARD H. SYLVESTER,
Superintendent of the Metropolitan Police Department,
Washington DC, 1910, as quoted in the *Report on Lawlessness in Law Enforcement* of the National Commission on Law Observance and Enforcement (Wickersham Commission), June 25, 1931

———

A confession is voluntary in law if, and only if, it was, in fact, voluntarily made . . . a confession obtained by compulsion must be excluded, whatever may have been the character of the compulsion and whether the compulsion was applied in a judicial proceeding or otherwise.

—Justice LOUIS D. BRANDEIS,
writing for a unanimous Supreme Court in the case of
Ziang Sung Wan v. United States, October 13, 1924

———

CONTENTS

LIST OF ILLUSTRATIONS

PREFACE

I SUSPECT THAT most story-behind-the-court-case books get their start when a landmark decision inspires a legal scholar to get to the root of a case, investigate the plaintiff's or defendant's story, and chart the rocky path through the judicial system of whatever point of law is at issue. Such books are compelling because people are naturally curious about the human story that drives a sweeping change in the law. As a college student, I devoured Anthony Lewis's award-winning *Gideon's Trumpet*, surely one of the great works in this genre. Even though I already knew how Clarence Gideon's case would get resolved, I thrilled in the events, so ably retold by Lewis, that got it to the Supreme Court, caused his conviction to be overturned, and extended the constitutional right to counsel to criminal defendants tried in state courts.

Lewis, then the *New York Times* reporter covering the Supreme Court beat, later confirmed that his interest in *Gideon v. Wainwright* began the day the Court agreed to hear the case. All signs pointed to the body's readiness to set an important legal precedent, and so he began his work even before the case was argued—reading up on existing law, shadowing the attorneys, and interviewing Gideon himself.[1]

This book began in precisely the *opposite* way. I am not an attorney, still less a legal scholar. I don't follow the Supreme Court any more closely than most Americans do. Like most everyone, I had never heard of Ziang Sung Wan, his alleged crime, his experience with the Washington DC police in 1919, or his court case, nor had I ever given much thought to the admissibility of confessions in criminal trials. I found my way to Wan not through his court case, but rather through the triple murder that gave rise to it. And I was half a year into my research before I fully grasped its implications.

In early 2015, on the lookout for a new story, I found myself on the Library of Congress's excellent *Chronicling America* website, a vast repository of historic American newspapers that have been digitized and rendered keyword-searchable by modern technology. This tool and others like it have enabled comprehensive research that would have been virtually impossible just a few years ago. Several of my earlier books owe their very existence to *Chronicling America* and its sister sites.

It was my hunt for a new story about the early Chinese experience in America that caused Ziang Sung Wan to pop up on my monitor one winter morning. I had casually entered two terms—"Chinese" and "murder"—into the search engine. And one of the first hits was the lead story in a 1919 edition of the *Washington Times*—not the modern paper, but an earlier broadsheet by the same name—that claimed that "the internationally famous triple Chinese murder mystery which has been agitating two continents" had been cracked.[2]

It got my attention.

That article led to many others—a couple of thousand, eventually—and before long I was hooked. The cold-blooded murder of three Chinese diplomats had baffled the Washington Police Department, made front page news in the capital, and garnered national attention. As I followed the story from the initial reports of the killings through the detention and interrogation of the principal suspect, his trial, his conviction, and his appeal, I learned that the case had ultimately made it all the way to the Supreme Court and that it had drawn the attention of Washington luminaries like Warren G. Harding, William Howard Taft, John W. Davis, Louis Brandeis, Oliver Wendell Holmes, George Wickersham, Charles Fahy, J. Edgar Hoover, and Earl Warren.

Ziang Sung Wan's story was a gripping tale, and I had resolved to tell it even before I discovered that it had laid the foundation for the Court's subsequent landmark *Miranda v. Arizona* decision. Far from working backwards from *Miranda*, I had begun almost a half century earlier and fortuitously wound up there.

In the process, I learned a great deal about a complex but fascinating area of constitutional law and explored how we got where we are today. The idea that people who are arrested have a right to remain silent and a right to counsel, and that they must be advised of these rights, was second nature to me, as it is to anyone in America who has ever watched an episode of *Law and Order* on television. But it was not always so. Not so very long ago, no such rights were presumed. Police officers felt no compunction against "sweating" confessions out of suspects and even resorting to torture, if necessary, to extract them.

The end was thought to justify the means.

Today we accept that the burden of proof rests squarely with law enforcement. Under the law, it is the responsibility of the police to gather evidence against a suspect without coercing the person into providing it. To do otherwise would be to violate the accused's rights, not to mention his or her dignity, and would in any case yield a highly suspect and potentially unreliable confession.

The convoluted journey that we as a nation made from a regime that viewed strong-arming suspects as both effective and proper to one that understands that it is neither took the better part of a century. The case of Ziang Sung Wan was an important way station on that rutted road. It was, in fact, a critical step that pointed the way toward the establishment of the safeguards and rights Americans cherish and take for granted today.

In the course of my investigation, I tried the patience of many attorney friends by peppering them with endless questions about criminal procedure. I camped out in archives and libraries and examined many original documents, puzzling through Justice Brandeis's handwritten notes and drafts and perusing the files of Wan's defense counsel, Charles Fahy. The curator of the Supreme Court approved my request for a peek at Justice Pierce Butler's 1923 docket book in which he had recorded the initial votes of his colleagues on the case; I even reviewed notes exchanged among the justices before the ruling was finalized.

I also met—online and in person—many generous people with personal connections to the century-old story. Several descendants of Theodore T. Wong, one of the murder victims, shared their knowledge and their unpublished family memoirs, becoming cherished friends in the process. My research even extended as far as Shanghai, where other friends helped me trace the footsteps of Ziang Sung Wan himself, who not only got his start but lived out his unhappy days there after his ordeal in America was over.

It has been a fascinating, edifying, and enjoyable journey. I am delighted to share what I have found.

A Note on Chinese Names

Most of the Chinese people mentioned in this book were originally from Shanghai. In the early twentieth century their names were romanized haphazardly according to the phonics of the Shanghainese dialect. In this work, I have employed the most common spellings used by the individuals themselves during their lifetimes. For clarity, however, in the *Dramatis Personae* section, I have also included both the modern pinyin spellings (which represent Mandarin pronunciations) and the standard Chinese characters (simplified characters were not yet in use during the period covered in the book) for the names, where I have been able to determine them, of the important Chinese figures. For other individuals, pinyin spelling, where known, follows the first mention in the book.

For Chinese place names, names of dynasties, and publications, I have generally used pinyin. In the few instances in which traditional spellings appear, I have indicated the pinyin spelling in parentheses immediately after the first mention.

DRAMATIS PERSONAE

Louis D. Brandeis

1856–1941

Associate Justice of the U.S. Supreme Court who penned the unanimous opinion in the case of *Ziang Sung Wan v. United States*.

Guy E. Burlingame

1868–1944

Police detective who participated in the murder investigation and the interrogation of Ziang Sung Wan and Tsong Ing Van.

Zechariah Chafee Jr.

1885–1957

Harvard Law School professor and civil libertarian who authored one of the final reports of the Wickersham Commission.

John W. Davis

1873–1955

Attorney, congressman, solicitor general, ambassador, and Democratic nominee for president who joined Wan's defense team in its appeal to the U.S. Supreme Court.

William Cullen Dennis

1878–1962

Attorney who was part of the team that appealed Ziang Sung Wan's case to the Supreme Court in 1923–24.

Charles Fahy

1892–1979

Washington DC criminal attorney who defended Ziang Sung Wan and his brother Tsong Ing Van from 1919 to 1924.

Peyton Gordon

1870–1946

United States attorney for the District of Columbia who opposed Ziang Sung Wan's appeal before the DC Court of Appeals and the Supreme Court.

Ashley M. Gould

1859–1921

Supreme Court of the District of Columbia judge who presided over the 1919–20 murder case against Ziang Sung Wan.

Clifford L. Grant

1865–1925

Chief of Detectives on the Washington police force who participated in the murder investigation and the interrogation of Ziang Sung Wan and Tsong Ing Van.

Warren G. Harding

1865–1923

President of the United States who refused even to consider commuting the sentence of Ziang Sung Wan in 1921.

Adolph A. Hoehling Jr.

1868–1941

Supreme Court of the District of Columbia judge who presided over the third trial of Ziang Sung Wan.

George D. Horning Jr.

1898–1974

Assistant United States attorney for the District of Columbia who served as prosecutor in Wan's 1926 retrials.

Chang Hsi Hsie (謝昌熙 **Xie Changxi**)

1884–1919

Treasurer of the Chinese Educational Mission and George Washington University student who was murdered in 1919.

Edward J. Kelly

1881–1946

Police detective who participated in the murder investigation and the interrogation of Ziang Sung Wan and Tsong Ing Van.

Wilton J. Lambert

1871–1935

Lawyer who defended Wan in his 1926 retrials before the Supreme Court of the District of Columbia.

John E. Laskey

1868–1945

United States attorney for the District of Columbia who prosecuted Ziang Sung Wan in his initial murder trial in 1919–20.

Bolitha J. Laws

1891–1958

Assistant U.S. attorney who helped prosecute the 1919–20 murder trial of Ziang Sung Wan.

Kang Li (李岡 Li Gang)

1896–aft. 1930

Physician and George Washington University student who discovered the bodies of the three murdered Chinese diplomats.

Frederic D. McKenney

1863–1949

Veteran attorney who was part of the legal team that represented Ziang Sung Wan before the U.S. Supreme Court.

Rev. Peter J. O'Callaghan

1866–1931

Catholic priest who enlisted several distinguished attorneys to defend Ziang Sung Wan on a *pro bono* basis.

Hugh A. O'Donnell

1874–1941

Newspaperman and onetime employer of Ziang Sung Wan who helped him secure *pro bono* counsel.

James A. O'Shea

1878–1949

Criminal attorney who represented Ziang Sung Wan and his brother Tsong Ing Van from 1919 to 1924.

Raymond W. Pullman

1883–1920

Chief of the Washington Police Department who oversaw the investigation of the Chinese Educational Mission murders.

Wendell P. Stafford

1861–1953

District of Columbia Supreme Court judge who presided over the second trial of Ziang Sung Wan.

A. Owsley Stanley

1867–1958

Former U.S. senator from Kentucky. An early critic of the third degree who joined Wan's defense team for the 1926 retrials.

William Howard Taft

1857–1930

Former president of the United States and chief justice of the U.S. Supreme Court who presided over the appeal of Ziang Sung Wan.

Tsong Ing Van (宦中英 Huan Zhongying)

1898–aft. 1950

Younger brother of Ziang Sung Wan who was charged with forgery but never tried for the crime.

Josiah Van Orsdel

1860–1937

District of Columbia Court of Appeals judge who ruled on Wan's case in 1923.

Ziang Sung Wan (宦祥生 Huan Xiangsheng)

1895–1968

Young man accused of killing three Chinese diplomats and convicted of one of the murders. Tried twice more after the Supreme Court overturned his conviction and eventually freed.

Kang Sung Wang

1896–19??

Friend of Ziang Sung Wan who met with him at a Washington DC police station immediately before he confessed to murder.

Earl Warren

1891–1974

Chief Justice of the U.S. Supreme Court who drafted the landmark opinion in the case of *Miranda v. Arizona*.

George W. Wickersham
1858–1936
Former attorney general of the United States who chaired a commission that exposed widespread abuse in police interrogation methods.

Theodore Ting Wong (黃佐庭 **Huang Zuoting**)
1876–1919
Shanghai-born, American-educated head of the Chinese Educational Mission who was murdered in 1919.

Ben Sen Wu (吳炳新 **Wu Bingxin**)
1898–1919
Secretary at the Chinese Educational Mission who was murdered in 1919, and may have been the killer of Theodore T. Wong and Chang Hsi Hsie.

THE THIRD DEGREE

Prologue

"The Best of Spirits Prevailed"

IT WAS TWO days before Chinese New Year, 1919, and the three men who made up the Chinese Educational Mission in Washington DC were all out for dinner.

Ringing in the Year of the Goat was a welcome break from the work of the mission, which had been established in 1911 to look after the hundreds of Chinese scholarship students studying at universities across the United States. It had been directed from the start by Theodore Ting Wong, forty-three, a Shanghai-born alumnus of the University of Virginia. A well-respected scholar adroit in both cultures, Wong was assisted by Chang Hsi Hsie, thirty-two, the organization's treasurer, an affable man who had served as registrar at China's Tsinghua (Qinghua) University before coming to the United States. The third man, the mission's secretary, was twenty-one-year-old Ben Sen Wu. Bright and sociable, he was a graduate of prestigious Peking (Beijing) University.

All three men were diplomats, although they were not domiciled at the Chinese Legation on 19th Street NW. Instead, they lived and worked a few minutes' walk away in a row house on Kalorama Road, just a few doors in from stately Connecticut Avenue. Hsie and Wu, scholarship recipients themselves, were also part-time students at George Washington University.

Dr. Wong and Mr. Hsie were dining at the upscale Nankin Restaurant on Ninth Street NW, guests of T. C. Quo (Guo Taiqi), a high-ranking Chinese diplomat passing through on his way to France. The fate of territories in China that had been controlled by Germany before World War I was to be discussed at the Paris Peace Conference, and Quo was serving as a technical adviser to the Chinese negotiators.

The host had arranged a sumptuous dinner for thirteen, replete with silver service and table linen, in a private room on the second floor of the restaurant, which advertised that it catered "only to the refined."[1] It was a congenial affair, and "the best of spirits prevailed throughout the evening," Quo said later.[2] The meal began at 7:00 p.m. and ended about three hours later.

Hsie left first, with a friend from the legation. The pair took a streetcar and got off three blocks from the mission at about 10:20 p.m. Declining an offer to return to the legation for a chat, he proceeded home.

At a few minutes after ten, Dr. Wong departed in the company of the host, his family members, and a secretary from the legation. He played with the Quos' little girl on the streetcar before the entire group got off at Connecticut Avenue and S Street NW. They walked a block to the Cordova Apartments, where the Quos were staying, and there they parted company at about 10:30 p.m. Then Dr. Wong made his way back to the mission, about ten minutes away on foot.

Wu, low on the mission's totem pole, had gone to a separate dinner. After class that Wednesday evening, he had headed for the Oriental Restaurant, a Pennsylvania Avenue chop suey joint just across from the municipal building. He had accepted an impromptu invitation from a fellow student, and they were joined by two friends. At dinner, Wu apologized to his classmate for having recently been so unavailable; he had been caring for a sick guest, he explained, who had taken up much of his time and energy but had finally returned to New York. After dinner, the quartet departed the restaurant just before 8:00 p.m., when Wu boarded a streetcar and returned to the mission.

Dr. Wong, Hsie, and Wu were never seen alive again.

1

Three Men in a Tub

THE SS *EMPRESS of Russia* had established herself as the Queen of the Pacific on her maiden voyage from Yokohama to Vancouver in 1913. Despite dense fog, blustery winds, and choppy seas, the nearly 600-foot British-built steamer made the journey in just nine days and five hours, shaving a full day off the previous record.

The "largest, fastest and most elegantly furnished" passenger steamship sailing the Pacific in its day, the liner had been fitted out to accommodate nearly three hundred passengers in first class, a hundred in second, and another eight hundred in steerage. It required a crew of 475 to operate. The first-class staterooms, arrayed around a grand staircase, featured sleeping berths fitted with brass bedsteads and private hot and cold water baths. Élite passengers paid as much as $225—more than $5,000 in today's currency and three times the cost of a steerage ticket—for passage from China to North America in comfort. For that fare they enjoyed the use of a 430-foot promenade, luxurious lounges, an opulent café, a writing room, a card room, a library, a gymnasium, and even a fully equipped dark room. And in quiet alcoves in the period-style dining hall, they supped on roast sirloin of beef, baked York ham, clear turtle soup, and herring roe on toast.[1]

If you had the money, this was surely the way to cross the ocean.

On April 8, 1916, the *Empress* discharged 356 passengers at Vancouver. About half were Chinese who had boarded in Hong Kong and Shanghai; these accounted for the lion's share of the steerage passengers. Few Chinese could afford to travel any other way. The vast majority were young Cantonese men, unskilled laborers bound ostensibly for Canada. If the opportunity presented itself, however, many no doubt hoped eventually to sneak across the border into the United States, where they might find work in the laundries and restaurants of San Francisco, New York, and other cities.

Subterfuge was necessary because of the Chinese Exclusion Act, which for more than three decades had forbidden the entry of Chinese workers into the United States. That 1882 Act of the U.S. Congress had slowed the number of legal Chinese immigrants to a trickle. It did not, however, apply to merchants, teachers, students, or diplomats, who were still permitted to enter freely. America wanted no more of China's laborers, but it was perfectly happy to accept her intelligentsia and her gentry.

Only seven Chinese were among the more than two hundred souls traveling in first class; these included two Washington DC–bound diplomats and a privately funded student heading for Ohio. The three knew one another; they were all Shanghainese and presented themselves together for examination by U.S. immigration officials conveniently stationed in Vancouver. These inspectors could bounce undesirables back to the Orient before they ever reached America. But the three Chinese men had little cause for worry. They were anything but migrant workers and they had no doubt they would be welcome.

The eldest of the trio was Dr. Theodore Ting Wong, quiet, balding, and bespectacled. He was on his third trip to the United States and was traveling at government expense. The scion of an unusual family with strong ties to America, Dr. Wong was heading back to resume his work at the Chinese Educational Mission after a year-long furlough. His associate, Chang Hsi Hsie, had been manning the organization in his absence.

Accompanying him on the *Empress* was Ben Sen Wu, who was coming for the first time. Like Wong, Wu came from privilege: his brother, chief of the treasury division of China's Ministry of Foreign Affairs, was a government official. Not yet eighteen, Wu did not know much English, but as one of the mission's scholarship students, he planned to improve his language skills and moonlight as a student at George Washington University.

The third man, who shared a stateroom with Wu, was traveling under somewhat different auspices. His name was Ziang Sung Wan and he was just shy of his twenty-first birthday. At nearly five foot ten he was relatively tall for a Chinese, but slender in build. Raised and educated in Shanghai, Wan also came from a well-to-do family with connections to the United States. His father had been one of the first 120 Chinese students ever to study abroad; the elder Wan had been sent to New England in the 1870s at age ten as part of a government-sponsored program—ironically also known as the Chinese Educational Mission. But after his return to China he had died at the age of thirty-five, leaving a widow with a sizeable estate and three boys and a girl to raise alone.[2]

Like the Wongs, the Wan family was Episcopalian; through the congregation in Shanghai, Dr. Wong had known Ziang Sung Wan since his childhood. Young Wan had attended Chant's Academy and St. John's College, both church-organized schools, so he spoke excellent English. Raised without a father, however, he was spoiled and undisciplined and had grown into something of a ne'er-do-well.

Wan's mother was worried about this son. She had begged Dr. Wong to take him to the United States to study in order to straighten him out, and to look out for him while he was there. She had paid for the young man's passage and given him funds to enroll in school once he arrived in America, since he was not a government scholarship recipient. Unlike that of his two shipmates, Wan's initial destination was not Washington but rather the Midwest, where his younger brother had preceded him.[3]

No one—least of all any of the three—could have predicted that, before four years had elapsed, two of them would be murdered in cold blood and the third would be accused of the crimes. Or that his arrest and trial would enthrall the capital city and capture national attention for several years. Nor could anyone possibly have foreseen that his case would ultimately reach the highest court in the land and establish an important legal principle.

It would take America a giant step forward toward guaranteeing the rights of criminal suspects and protecting them from abusive interrogation at the hands of police across the nation.

2

An Unwelcome Guest

APPROXIMATELY 350 GOVERNMENT-FUNDED Chinese students were studying in the United States when Dr. Wong and Ben Sen Wu arrived in Washington in 1916. They were attending some of America's best schools, including Cornell, MIT, Columbia, the University of Michigan, Harvard, George Washington, and the University of Pennsylvania. Their expenses were paid from a scholarship fund created from money the Chinese government had been forced to pay to the U.S. government following the Boxer Rebellion of 1899–1901.[1]

A violent, xenophobic uprising in which many foreign missionaries, merchants, and diplomats lost life and property, that rebellion had enjoyed tacit government support; when it was finally suppressed by an international military force, the Qing regime—China's Manchu government—was compelled to pay reparations to the governments of eight foreign countries. These took the form of a $333 million indemnity, payable in installments. America's share was just over seven percent: about $24 million, or more than $500 million in today's dollars.

It soon became clear, however, that America's losses amounted to only about half of that sum, so discussions began about returning the surplus to China. President Theodore Roosevelt was willing to do this, but he was persuaded to set terms for how the money was to be spent. These conditions were benevolent: they called for establishing schools in China and for sending Chinese students abroad. Once the enabling legislation passed Congress in 1908, the first remittance was made. And when the Qing dynasty fell in 1912, its successor government—the Republic of China—assumed its obligations and continued the program.[2]

Boxer indemnity funds underwrote the 1911 establishment in Beijing of Tsinghua Imperial College—later Tsinghua University—whose early mission was to prepare Chinese students for study in America. Young Chinese men—and, beginning in 1916, women as well—were sent to the United States at the rate of about fifty a year; over the life of the program, more than 1,200 students were supported.[3]

Theodore Wong had been an excellent choice to manage this program, not only because he was well regarded as a scholar—he had authored a compendium of the Chinese dynasties and edited a Chinese-English dictionary—but also because he was outgoing and genial and possessed a near-native command of English. Perhaps most importantly, he was well connected in China and wise in the ways of America. His father, the Reverend Kong Chai Wong, had been the first convert of the American Episcopal Church in Shanghai as well its first Chinese deacon and its first Chinese priest. He had also been one of the first recorded Chinese visitors to the southern United States when he traveled there with an American missionary in 1843. His wife, Theodore's mother, had been the first Chinese girl in Shanghai to receive baptism.[4]

Theodore—the ninth of ten children, only six of whom survived to adulthood, and the only son—had thus been raised Christian, which was rare in late nineteenth century China. He had grown up around foreigners. He had also prepared at St. John's College—later St. John's University—and had first sailed for the United States in 1892 to continue his studies, initially at Episcopal High School in Alexandria, Virginia, and later at the University of Virginia in Charlottesville. There he read Greek, Latin, history, English, natural philosophy, and political economy. He finished his studies in 1896.

By 1898 he had returned to China, where he married Julia Sih (Xue Pa), one of the first students at the McTyeire School, a girls' academy established in Shanghai by Methodist missionaries in 1892. He was twenty-two—it was time to begin a family. Beginning in 1899, Julia bore five daughters, followed by two sons. It was a happy household, their daughter Ethel recalled, "always full of laughter." Wong was light on his feet and there were frequent dancing parties and social gatherings. The children enjoyed a life of leisurely vacations, imported foodstuffs, and European- and American-made toys.

FIG. 1. Dr. Theodore T. Wong. Courtesy of Wade Wei Loo.

A modest man, Wong first became a teacher. He was also active in the Chinese Red Cross and served as the first president of the Shanghai YMCA. In 1909, he had been named chief secretary of the new Shanghai-Nanking (Nanjing) Railroad and, at the end of 1911, leaving his family behind, he had been sent to Washington to supervise the overseas students supported by the Chinese Educational Mission.[5] He was in America when the boy emperor Pu Yi abdicated the throne and the Republic of China was established; he remained in the United States until 1915, when he took home leave in China for a reunion with his family.

In Washington, Wong had initially rented an apartment on Columbia Road in the northwest quadrant of the city, living and working there with Chang Hsi Hsie, the organization's treasurer. Hsie, also a St. John's graduate, was a steady hand who watched the money and kept the organization on track. He had served the foreign ministry in its Yokohama consulate before becoming registrar at Tsinghua and had arrived in the United States two years earlier.[6]

It was a good time to be away from China. The new democracy had gotten off to a decidedly shaky start. Yuan Shih Kai (Yuan Shikai), who had assumed the presidency, soon waged war with his political adversaries, dissolved the national assembly, and actually briefly proclaimed himself emperor. There was a revolt against him in the south. Warlords in several provinces maintained local militias and governed with little regard for the central authorities. Japan, already occupying part of Manchuria and the former German colony at Qingdao and hungry for more territory, had just presented China with a secret set of twenty-one demands that would essentially turn the country into a vassal state.

War was also very much on people's minds in Washington. Woodrow Wilson, who had won the presidency three years earlier, was running for re-election on the slogan "He kept us out of war," but America would not be able to stay out much longer. Domestically, Wilson pushed a progressive agenda and appointed officials to match. Among them was John W. Davis, known popularly as "the lawyer's lawyer," who was named solicitor general in 1913. Although he was a political conservative who opposed women's suffrage, he supported progressive initiatives aimed at limiting the power of big business. As a congressman from West Virginia, he had been one of the authors of the Clayton Antitrust Act, which aimed to curb anticompetitive practices in the corporate world. During the first five years of the Wilson administration, Davis gained valuable experience as the government's chief litigator, arguing constitutional cases before the Supreme Court.

Another Wilson appointee was attorney Louis D. Brandeis, known, by contrast, as "the people's lawyer," for the time and energy he devoted to public causes and his commitment to social justice. Wilson's choice of Brandeis for a seat on the Supreme Court in 1916 was so controversial that he became the first candidate in the history of the court whose nomination was subjected to confirmation hearings in the Senate—a blistering, four-month process that had more to do with his Judaism than it did his judicial philosophy.

The capital city was undergoing a massive makeover, inspired by the City Beautiful movement, which sought to spruce up urban America and promote civic virtue and social order in the process. Victoriana was out; the campaign emphasized classical architecture and open spaces. The McMillan Plan, formulated by a senate commission at the beginning of the century, had dictated the destruction of vast tracts of slums, the reclamation of land for waterfront parks, and the creation of grand vistas. Union Station, the gleaming white neoclassical rail terminal designed by architect Daniel Burnham, had risen in 1908 and anticipated the construction of similar edifices. And Congress would soon appropriate funds for renovation of the Old City Hall, which had, since the Civil War, housed the District of Columbia courts. The Judiciary Square structure was to be stripped to its brick framing and its exterior stucco replaced with neoclassical white limestone.

Washington was growing rapidly. Between 1910 and 1920, its population increased by a third to more than 430,000. But only the affluent could afford to live in Kalorama, a tony northwest neighborhood just north of the original city limits in which Wong rented a townhouse in 1916 for Hsie, Wu, and himself to live and work. Located at 2023 Kalorama Road, just half a block from Connecticut Avenue, the ten-room, brick-and-stone row house, which he leased for $60 a month, was a short walk from the Chinese Legation on 19th Street.

President Warren G. Harding, then a U.S. senator from Ohio, would buy a house in that neighborhood the following year and remain in it until his inauguration in 1921. That same year, Herbert Hoover would move to the neighborhood and stay until he, too, packed up for 1600 Pennsylvania Avenue. Former president William Howard Taft would purchase a home there as he assumed the position of chief justice of the United States. John Edgar Hoover, a Justice Department attorney who would soon become head of the Bureau of Investigation's new General Intelligence Division, lived a few doors from the mission. All these men would play important roles in the drama that would follow from events that occurred at the new mission offices on a winter's night in 1919.

The District of Columbia also had a tiny but well-established Chinatown. Like most of the Chinese quarters in the cities of the East and Midwest, it had gotten its start in the 1870s, when Chinese from the West began migrating eastward in growing numbers to search for work and to flee bigotry and violence against them that had burgeoned after the completion of the Transcontinental Railroad. Washington was home to approximately 400 Chinese—mostly laundrymen, cigar-makers, restaurateurs, and grocers—and the bulk lived on, or adjacent to, a short, run-down stretch of Pennsylvania Avenue near the Capitol between 3rd and 7th Streets NW. Like the Chinese population elsewhere in America, Washington's Chinatown was predominantly Cantonese and overwhelmingly male.

Wong and his associates probably bought provisions from these Chinese and certainly ate at their restaurants, but they lived three miles away and surely considered themselves a breed apart. They were highly educated and fluent English speakers, whereas most local Chinese were neither. They were Shanghainese, speaking a dialect unintelligible to the Cantonese. They were government officials from a cosmopolitan city who came from privilege, not former peasants and shopkeepers from rural villages in a far corner of the empire. They hobnobbed with upper-class Americans, while those in Chinatown washed their shirts. Wong and Wu had traveled to America in a first-class cabin; few residents of Chinatown could make a similar claim.

As a member of the diplomatic corps, Dr. Wong enjoyed entrée to the "smart set," patrician Washingtonians who would never have dreamed of befriending the denizens of Chinatown. His was a life of formal dinners, receptions, and speeches. Shortly before Holy Week

ZIANG-SUNG WEN, A. B.
  SHANGHAI, CHINA

C. P. S., Tientsin, C. A., Shanghai
S. J. U. Shanghai
Chinese Student Alliance U. S.A.
Cosmopolitan Club
Adelphian

FIG. 2. 1917 yearbook entry for Ziang-Sung Wen [*sic*]. Source: *The Northern.*
Courtesy of Heterick Memorial Library-ONU Archives.

of 1913, for example, he was invited to speak at the Waugh Methodist
Episcopal Church at Third and A Streets NE. And Wellington Koo,
China's minister to the United States, feted him at a dinner after his
return in 1916. Koo, also Shanghainese and a St. John's alumnus, was
an old friend who had studied at Columbia University before returning to China to become English secretary to President Yuan Shih Kai.[7]

Life in America was proving quite different for Wong's shipmate,
young Ziang Sung Wan, who had joined his brother Tsong Ing Van,
younger by three years, in Ohio. Van—who had romanized their surname differently from his brother, both spellings being reasonable
approximations of the Shanghainese pronunciation—had begun his
studies there the previous year.

Slightly stocky and shorter than his brother by two inches, Van had
entered Ohio Wesleyan University in Delaware, Ohio, at the age of
seventeen and pursued the classical course. He studied Greek, Latin,
mathematics, and chemistry. His elder brother headed to Ada, fifty-
eight miles to the northwest, and enrolled in the liberal arts program
at Ohio Northern University. Wan was listed in its 1917 yearbook as
having earned a bachelor of arts degree. Since he studied there for
only a year, this suggests that courses he had taken at St. John's in
China were counted toward the degree. Because it was registered in
Washington DC, St. John's enjoyed the status of a domestic university, and its credits were transferable.

By June 1917 Wan had left Ohio for New York City. The country had entered the First World War; all men between the ages of twenty-one and thirty-one, aliens included, were required to register for the draft, although foreigners were not asked to serve. Wan did so in mid-1917, listing himself as a student. He was living on the Upper West Side, in the Morningside Heights neighborhood adjacent to Columbia University, and later maintained that he had studied at the college in the summer of 1918, although the school can find no record of him today. Nor is there a trace of his brother matriculating at Columbia, though he declared as much on his own draft registration form, completed in New York the following summer. Van had left Ohio before graduating. He rented a furnished room from a widow named Gertrude Bartels in the rear of 313 W. 112th Street, a block from Morningside Park. After several months, his elder brother moved in with him there.[8]

The young men were still being supported by their mother, who sometimes sent money directly and sometimes through the good offices of Dr. Wong in Washington. But they also made efforts to bring in some income on their own. Wan, always immaculately groomed and presentable, briefly took a position as valet to a well-known newspaperman named Hugh A. O'Donnell, who took a liking to the young Chinese man and would later prove a most valuable friend. The job involved seeing to O'Donnell's mail and other menial tasks. The two men developed a good rapport, but Wan didn't last long in the position for two reasons.

First, as O'Donnell recalled much later, the superstitious Wan took exception to a cat's-eye stickpin O'Donnell had received as a gift. He imagined the gemstone to be a powerful amulet of which he was very much afraid. But the second reason was far more practical: Wan contracted the Spanish flu, becoming a victim of the great influenza pandemic that took the lives of an estimated 30,000 New Yorkers and tens of millions of people worldwide between 1918 and 1919. He was fortunate that it did not kill him, but it made him exceedingly uncomfortable and sapped him of his strength for many months.[9]

In July 1918 Wan received checks from Shanghai totaling $2,000, intended for tuition. He had no bank account, so he asked a friend to introduce him to the U.S. Mortgage and Trust Company, where he deposited the funds. But he and his brother had other plans for the money. In early September he withdrew half the sum to invest in a shaky business proposition. He leased a moving-picture theater in Brooklyn from a man named Israel Weinberg. Wan agreed to pay Weinberg $1,000 in cash at the time of signing and an additional $500 the following May from expected proceeds from the business.

Van then left for Providence, Rhode Island, where he secured a short-term job in a munitions plant, leaving Wan to run the business—by one account with additional investment from Ben Sen Wu, his shipmate and friend who was working for Dr. Wong in Washington. Wan knew nothing about the movie business, however. Weinberg was supposed to teach him how to operate the theater. He moved to Brooklyn and made a good-faith effort to get it up and running, plowing more of his money into repairs. The hall was open for only two or three weeks, however. By the time Van returned to New York in late October, Wan could not come up with a $200 rent payment and the enterprise was shuttered. Unable to sell the lease, he simply walked away from the venture and moved back to 112th Street. Most of the money was gone.[10]

Ignorant of the theater scheme, Wan's mother sent another $500 in October via the Washington mission; the men received $200 more as a Christmas present from their sister's husband. Dr. Wong visited New York at Christmas and asked Wan to meet him at the Hotel Marseille, perhaps to pass along this money or one of the packages his mother occasionally sent in care of Washington. But the relationship with Dr. Wong was not an easy one: the brothers likely perceived him as something of a scold. According to one of Wong's daughters, there was often friction over their behavior and spending habits.[11]

The Christmas money was soon gone. Wan was now not only ill; he was also broke. His account at U.S. Mortgage had only $41.07 left in it. And he had not been getting along at all well with his brother, who was again sharing quarters with him. He received a telegram from his friend Wu, urging him to spend the holidays at the mission in Washington, but he was too sick to go. For two weeks he lived on little more than black coffee and toast. Wu, concerned, sent him a check for $50 and continued to urge him to visit. "You are not attending the school," he wrote, "and you can spend your time in Washington just the same as in New York."

Then in mid-January 1919, still complaining of an upset stomach, Wan began to self-medicate with whiskey. His landlady noticed it and urged him to check himself into a hospital, but he stubbornly refused and the two had words. Finally the argument came to a head.

"All right. If you do not want me in your house anymore, I will get out," he told her. And the next day, Wednesday, January 22, he boarded a train for Washington.[12]

After arriving at Union Station, he headed for the Chinese Educational Mission, a narrow, brick row house three miles away, decorated tastefully with rich oriental carpets, tapestries, and furniture that was a blend of East and West. Built in 1900, it had three bedrooms and a bath on the third floor. Dr. Wong occupied the front room, Wu the middle, and Hsie the rear chamber. The front parlor on the second floor served the men as a sitting room; behind it was a guest bedroom, where Wan was invited to lodge. It had recently been vacated by a young man named Kang Li, a Chinese physician studying at George Washington University with Hsie and Wu under the supervision of the mission. Li had stayed there for about a week while a visiting Chinese woman occupied his quarters across the street at 2041 Kalorama. In the rear was a bathroom and Hsie's office. Dr. Wong worked out of the back room on the ground floor. Adjoining it was his reception hall and in the very front a salon with a large, curved bay looking out on Kalorama Road. A kitchen shared the basement with the furnace room.

Wan stayed at the mission for five days. Because of his illness, Wu moved downstairs to the second floor to keep him company during the nights. But the mission had no servants and Wan decided to go home. He explained later that he felt uncomfortable inconveniencing Wu and his colleagues, especially at the end of the month when everyone was busy mailing out scholarship checks. Another explanation is that there was friction between him and others at the house. Theodore Wong did not entirely approve of him; Wan may have felt his continued presence was unwanted, even by Wu. On Monday,

B. S. WU   C. H. HSIE

Fig. 3. Ben Sen Wu and Chang Hsi Hsie.
Source: *The Chinese Students' Monthly*.

January 27, he lunched with Wu at Breslau's Delicatessen and Lunch-room near 18th Street and Columbia Road, and angry words passed between them, the Washington *Evening Star* reported much later, without citing a source.[13]

Wan didn't make it to New York that day. Instead, he checked into the Harris Hotel at Massachusetts Avenue and North Capitol Street. He chose it because it was just a block from Union Station, where he would eventually board a train to return to New York. Plus, rooms there were relatively cheap, starting at only $1.50 a night.

The first thing he did after moving into the Harris was to dispatch a telegram to his brother in New York. He sent another later in the day and two more the following day, summoning his sibling to his bed-side. Van initially hesitated but, sensing his brother's urgency, finally hurried to Washington, arriving by train at 1:00 a.m. on the morning of Wednesday, January 29. As Van would later tell the story, he discovered his brother in extreme distress, experiencing pain in his abdomen, but unable to void. Van went out and purchased a syringe, filled it with hot water, soap, and a teaspoonful of turpentine and administered a makeshift enema, which provided some relief. He also went to Chinatown to find some canned fruit, which his brother fancied.[14]

But Wan was not too sick to make a trip back to the mission; he explained later that he went to fetch a package Wu said had arrived for him from China. Later that day his brother helped him dress and he left the hotel at about 6:00 p.m., alone. An hour or so later, Kang Li, Ben Sen Wu's classmate, happened to ring the doorbell at the Kalorama house. He wanted to consult Wu about a letter he had just received. There was no immediate answer, but Li saw a light in the front hallway and, peering through the front window, spotted Wan's derby hat and muffler on the coat rack. He knew Wan, although not well; he had met him on a few occasions while the latter was a guest at the mission. But as far as he knew, Wan had already returned to New York.

The hat and scarf were an unmistakable sign that someone was home, so Li continued to knock. Eventually, Wan came to the door, opening it only about a foot and pointedly not inviting Li in.

"Is Mr. Wu at home?" Li asked.

"He has gone out," Wan replied.

"Is Dr. T. T. Wong home?"

"He has gone out," was the answer.[15]

The whole situation seemed odd. Li knew that Wan had moved out of the mission two days earlier to return to Manhattan, yet suddenly he was back and apparently there all alone. His manner was curt. But Li accepted the rebuff and went away. There was really nothing else to do.

In fact, none of the three diplomats *was* at the mission at 7:00 p.m. that night. Everyone had gone out for dinner to celebrate the Chinese New Year.

After class, Ben Sen Wu had joined friends at the Oriental Restaurant on Pennsylvania Avenue. Wu explained his recent unavailability: a recent guest—Ziang Sung Wan—had taken up much of his time, but had finally left town. The party departed the restaurant at 7:50 p.m., after which Wu returned to the mission by streetcar.

For their part, Dr. Wong and Mr. Hsie were dining at the Nankin Restaurant on Ninth Street NW as guests of T. C. Quo, on his way to the Paris Peace Conference. Organized to establish the terms of the post–World War I peace, the conference involved nearly thirty countries. Of paramount importance to China was whether Japan, per its twenty-one demands, would be granted territories in China that had been controlled by Germany before the war.

The farewell dinner for thirteen in a private room on the second floor of the restaurant included several diplomats from the Chinese Legation. It ended at about 10:00 p.m. Hsie left first with a friend from the legation. The pair took a Mt. Pleasant streetcar and got off three blocks from the mission at about 10:20 p.m. Then Hsie proceeded home.

Dr. Wong departed soon after, in the company of the host, his wife, her sister, and a secretary from the legation. The five also boarded a streetcar and got off at Connecticut Avenue and S Street NW, where they walked a block to the Cordova Apartments, the Quos' temporary residence. They parted at about 10:30 p.m., after which Dr. Wong, in good spirits, made his way back to the mission, less than ten minutes away on foot.

Van spent the night with his brother at the hotel. The following day, Thursday, January 30, at a little after nine in the morning, the brothers hailed a taxicab at Union Station and headed for Riggs National Bank, just across the street from the White House. While Wan remained in the cab, his brother entered the cavernous lobby and presented a teller with an envelope containing a $5,000 check, drawn on the account of the Chinese Educational Mission. Made payable to "bearer," it bore the signatures of both T. T. Wong and C. H. Hsie. The envelope also included a note to the bank on mission stationery with the same signatures, requesting that the bank make payment to the carrier.

Something about the check looked odd to the teller; it was unusual for such a large amount to be made payable simply to "bearer." When he compared the signatures to those on an earlier, paid check from the mission's account, he became even more suspicious and turned the matter over to George O. Vass, an assistant cashier. Van was invited

FIG. 4. Riggs National Bank, ca. 1919. Source: Library of Congress, LC-USZ62-17956.

to speak with the officer, at which point he produced Ben Sen Wu's business card and suggested that the bank telephone the mission for instructions. Several attempts were made to reach North 1480, the mission's number, but no one answered.[16]

Finally, Van was told that the only way he could receive the funds would be for Dr. Wong to come to the bank and identify him personally. Vass returned the check and Van left the bank. He and Wan returned to Union Station and by 5:00 p.m. were back in New York, where Van helped his sick brother undress and put him to bed. He also went out and bought him some chicken and fish, which the landlady graciously cooked for him. Wan spent the next day—Friday, January 31—in bed.

Back in Washington, things were starting to stack up at the mission. At 9:00 a.m. on Thursday morning, when the mailman rang to deliver a piece of registered mail to Dr. Wong, no one answered. This was unusual; there was always activity there. What was even more peculiar was that both the morning paper and the milk remained on the steps. The postman returned at 12:30 and again at 3:15, but still no one answered. He even tried the door, which was usually open, but found it locked.

The next day, when he attempted on three separate occasions to deliver the mail, another newspaper and a second bottle of milk had appeared.

Something was very wrong.

3

Murder at the Mission

Tsu-Li Sun, an attaché at the Chinese Legation on Nineteenth Street, was studying at George Washington University together with Hsie and Wu; all three were enrolled in a course on banking. He hadn't seen either man since Tuesday, however, which was odd. So late in the afternoon of Friday the 31st, as he was passing the mission on Kalorama Road, he decided to stop and knock on their door again.

When he got up the steps, he noticed not only the unread newspapers and the milk but also a package of laundry that had been delivered to the house, all still unattended. After he rang the bell and got no answer, he crossed the street to number 2041 to see if Kang Li knew where the men had gone.

Li didn't, nor had he seen any of them since before Wednesday night, when he had stood on the front steps and been told by Ziang Sung Wan that they were all away. Reminded of the mystery, he crossed the street at about 6:00 p.m. and once again rang the bell, to no avail. The door was still locked but he noticed that one of the three front windows in the bay of the first floor salon was open about half an inch. He was able to raise the bottom pane and propel himself from the front steps into the room. Due to the lateness of the hour and the time of year, everything was dark; all he could make out was a pile of letters on the floor of the vestibule pushed through the mail slot by the postman. Having stayed at the mission himself for several days, however, he more or less knew his way around and quickly located the light switch in the front hall.

As he flicked it on, the light revealed the outline of a man's foot, motionless on the floor of the hall at the foot of the stairs.

Terrified, he didn't dare look any further. He rushed out, dashed across the road, and telephoned Sun at the legation. He told him something terrible had happened at the mission and pleaded with him to call the police immediately. Then he bounded back into the street and, with the aid of a newsboy, flagged down an officer and led him back to the mission. They were soon joined by several detectives and patrolmen summoned by Sun.

Li accompanied the police as they entered the reception hall. An officer lifted the overcoat draped over the face of the corpse; Li recognized the body as that of Dr. Wong. A deep, two-inch gash marred his forehead and there were abrasions on the top and back of his head. Two gunshot wounds had pierced his torso, one through the heart and the other in the armpit; the scorch marks on his vest testified to the fact that he had been shot at close range. Furniture had been overturned. A heavy brass lamp and the shattered remains of its shade and bulb lay on the floor near the body, suggesting that a scuffle had taken place.[1]

A crimson trail led down the basement stairway. The narrow stairwell descended into a kitchen in disarray, bearing evidence of a bloody struggle. On the floor was a handkerchief embroidered with the name "Wong" and, on a nearby chair, a .32-caliber revolver. But it was the furnace room that served up the most gruesome sight: the decomposing corpses of Hsie and Wu, lying head to head on the floor. Like Dr. Wong, the two were fully clothed. Hsie's face had been covered with a pillowcase, but not Wu's. Hsie had been shot once through his head and Wu twice, in his head and his heart.

The obvious first step for the police was to interview Kang Li; he had known all the victims well and had been the one to discover Dr. Wong's body. Led by Major Raymond W. Pullman, the chief of the department, they questioned the Chinese man thoroughly that evening. A onetime newspaperman, the thirty-five-year-old Pullman had been in office since 1915; he was the youngest police chief in any of the nation's large cities. He had a reputation for rectitude, conscientiousness, and tenacity: "He never stops until his task is completed—and then he begins on something else," one of his men once said of him.

FIG. 5. 2023 Kalorama Road NW, Washington DC.
Source: *Washington Times.*

Patient, tactful, and indefatigable, he was popular with the police force and well regarded in the city generally.[2]

Li was cooperative, if somewhat naïve, in his responses.

"Have you ever seen the murder gun before?" Pullman asked him.

"Yes," Li replied.

"Where?"

"Wu showed it to me once some time ago."

"Do you know where he kept it?"

"Yes, in his desk."

"Do you know where he kept the cartridges?"

"Yes, in the drawer of the table downstairs."

Li added of his own accord that Wu had once shown him how to fire the pistol; it was rusty and took some strength to discharge. He also allowed that he had only recently returned the front door key he had been given while staying at the mission. He identified the bodies of Hsie and Wu and recalled for the officers that Dr. Wong had had some enemies: he had received threatening letters during a trip to San Francisco the previous November and had switched hotels and hired a bodyguard as precautionary measures while there.[3]

In response to questions about the murdered men's recent activities and associations, Li told them about the visit of Ziang Sung Wan and about his mysterious encounter with Wan at the mission the previous Wednesday—two days after the latter had supposedly returned to New York.

This struck Major Pullman as a promising lead; in fact, it was the *only* lead they had. So he directed Detective Sergeants Guy E. Burlingame and Edward J. Kelly to travel immediately to New York and pick Wan up for questioning. Burlingame, fifty-two, had been with the force since 1896 and had handled some of the department's most difficult cases. He was credited with collaring a safe-blower and jewel thief whose arrest had been one of the most important in the department's history. And the thirty-six-year-old Kelly, appointed in 1906 and promoted to detective in 1915, was considered one of the department's most skilled investigators.[4]

A discarded package wrapper found at the mission provided Wan's address: 313 W. 112th Street in Manhattan. Realizing they might need help identifying the Chinese man, the detectives asked Kang Li to come along with them, even though they had not ruled him out as a suspect. He readily agreed and the trio boarded a midnight train for New York. Some time on the ride up, however, it dawned on Li that he himself was a person of interest in the investigation.

At seven thirty the following morning—Saturday, February 1—the

FIG. 6. A view of the body of Dr. Theodore T. Wong in situ
at the crime scene. Source: *Washington Times.*

men pulled up in a taxi in front of Mrs. Bartels's boarding house,
escorted by a New York police officer. Before they proceeded to Wan's
room, they asked his landlady whether he had lately been out of
town; she told them he had left her house about January 22 and not
returned until the day before. She also confirmed that his brother
Van had not been at home on Wednesday and that she had not seen
him again until Thursday afternoon. Then she led the men to Wan's
room on the top floor, where they dismissed her.

Ordering Kang Li to remain out of sight in the hallway, Burlingame and Kelly knocked on the door of the brothers' room. Van
and Wan were both there. Burlingame announced that they were
detectives from Washington investigating the deaths of Dr. Theodore Wong, Mr. Chang Hsi Hsie, and Mr. Ben Sen Wu, and then
they entered the room.

As Burlingame remembered it, Wan exchanged glances with his
brother but expressed no surprise at the news of the deaths. He was

sitting up in bed in his underwear and a sweater, and announced that he had already read about the murders in the morning papers. In fact, he was in the process of drafting a condolence telegram to the Chinese Legation in Washington. He handed Burlingame a piece of note paper on which the words "shocked to read of the death" had been written. Wan then asked the detectives all about the murders: when and where the men had been killed, when the bodies had been discovered, and whether the killer had been found. He expressed astonishment and grief at the death of his "good friends" and speculated that the murders might have been the work of the tongs—Chinatown gangs with a reputation for violent, Chinese-on-Chinese crime.

The detectives had questions for Wan as well, of course, but they made no mention of the possibility that at some future time his answers might be used against him in court, nor were they obligated to do so. They asked when he had left Washington. Burlingame later swore that he had initially answered Monday the 27th, but that once Kang Li was invited into the room, he immediately changed his answer to the 29th, the day Li had seen him on the doorstep of the mission. If true, it was not an auspicious beginning to his interrogation. But neither Van nor Wan remembered it that way.

As the brothers recalled it, the detectives entered the room with guns drawn, patted Van down, and demanded that Wan hand over his pistol, even though he did not possess one. Without benefit of a search warrant, Kelly rifled through the bureau and Wan's trunk while Burlingame pulled at the bed sheets and ripped open the mattress looking for a weapon, prompting Van to caution him not to treat his sick brother so roughly. Kelly then threatened to order Van out of the room. But once the detectives had determined that there was no weapon on the premises, the atmosphere grew less tense and Wan answered their questions. According to him, he never said anything other than that he had left the capital on the 29th.

Wan expressed a wish to go to Washington to provide whatever help he might be able to give the police in their investigation but his offer wasn't sincere. He immediately followed it with a protest that he had no money for such a trip and that, in any event, he was too sick to go: his stomach was upset and he required medical attention.

Burlingame promised to take care of his expenses and accommodate him in all of these respects if he would go. Li, a doctor, chimed in as well, volunteering to help nurse him while he was in the capital.

Li urged him to make the trip, pointing out that the victims had been good friends of theirs and that the police already knew he had seen Wan at the mission on Wednesday. In fact, the two of them, as far as Li knew, were the last to have been at the house. He pleaded for Wan's help to clear things up because, he observed, both he *and* Wan were suspects in the case. At this point, over Van's objection that he was too weak to make the journey, Wan consented to be dressed. He washed his face and brushed his teeth, while Van helped him pack a few items into a suitcase. Van offered to accompany him, but the detectives said he would not be needed. Then Wan left with Li and the detectives.

The group went first to a local police station, where Burlingame placed a long-distance call to Major Pullman to inform him they had found Wan and would be arriving in Washington with him at about 6:00 p.m. Pullman promised to dispatch a police car to the rail yards so the party could avoid Union Station, where he predicted reporters and curiosity-seekers would be awaiting their arrival. Then the party took a car to Pennsylvania Station, where they boarded a train for Washington.[5]

While the two detectives were in New York, their colleagues in Washington continued searching the premises. The coroner had come to some initial conclusions in his autopsies, a police photographer had recorded the crime scene from various angles, and a fingerprint expert had dusted the presumed murder weapon and other surfaces for prints. The police began to develop theories of the crime.

There was no sign of forced entry. Neighbors had heard shots but disagreed as to the time. The autopsy, however, revealed that the men had been dead more than thirty-six hours, which established the probable time of death as some time between noon and midnight on Wednesday, January 29. The coroner also found that all three had been shot to death with the .32-caliber revolver Li had identified as belonging to Wu.

A total of nine bullets had been recovered by the police, five of

FIG. 7. Major Raymond W. Pullman (*front row, fifth from right*), chief of police of the District of Columbia, posing with a group of police captains, ca. 1915. Source: Library of Congress, LC-F81-2371.

which had penetrated the three bodies. But three chambers in the rusty pistol were still loaded; the rest were empty, suggesting that the gun had been reloaded between murders, presumably by someone familiar enough with the premises to know where the bullets were kept. There were fingerprints on the pistol and on the lampshade, but all proved too indistinct to be useful. No government documents appeared to have been disturbed. Dr. Wong's pockets still contained his billfold, his watch, and some jewelry, which seemed to rule out theft as a motive for his murder.

A business card from Police Detective Charles H. Bradley was found on one of the tables. Bradley had visited the mission the previous July, when Dr. Wong had been so disturbed by the pilfering of office supplies and stamp money from the petty cash box that he had called the police and had the locks changed on the doors to the house and to his office. But Bradley had also called at the mission at about 9:00 p.m. on the day of the murders in response to a second summons earlier in the week. Although he saw a light burning on one of the upper floors, no one had answered the door, so he wrote a short note on the back of his card that he had called and would be back the next day, pushed it through the mail slot, and left.[6]

The police thought the fact that the faces of two of the slain men had been covered up was significant and that it pointed to a Chinese murderer. "It is an ancient Chinese custom," Burlingame later opined with an air of authority, "immediately to cover the face of the dead, be it natural or accidental death—or murder."[7] And they believed that Chinese killers, as a rule, tended to flee a city after their work was done. This observation was likely drawn from the tong wars, when triads often imported compatriots from other cities to do their dirty work on the assumption that they could more easily escape detection. This fact, in the minds of the police, tended to exonerate Li, who had remained in Washington, and point toward Wan.

By this time, the police had been informed by Riggs Bank about the $5,000 check that had been presented for payment on Thursday by an unknown Chinese man.[8] They suspected it was Wan who had tried to cash it but could not be certain without positive identification.

Major Pullman was right to worry about publicity. Despite a gag order imposed on those involved in the investigation, the Washington press had already learned all about Burlingame and Kelly's trip. The *Washington Times* even published the name of Ziang Sung Wan in its evening edition that day. The murder of the three Chinese diplomats would be front-page news in the nation's capital for many days hence; reporters from Washington's four major newspapers—to say nothing of those from the out-of-town papers that covered the story—could be counted on to grasp at every nugget offered them and to speculate in the absence of facts.[9]

Dozens of people—reporters, photographers, and gapers—had gathered at Union Station to get a glimpse of Wan but the police foiled them by avoiding the passenger concourse entirely. Wan and his escorts exited through the rear of the train; all but Li boarded a patrol car a distance from the station. From there they were ferried not to police headquarters, where Pullman knew reporters would also be waiting, but rather to the Board of Police Surgeons health clinic at 409 Fifteenth Street NW, where he knew they would not be disturbed. Pullman met them himself, together with his right-hand man, fifty-four-year-old Inspector Clifford L. Grant, the chief of detectives. Grant was known for his ability to get obstinate people to talk.

Wan greeted Pullman obsequiously. "I am very glad to make your acquaintance, Major," he said. "I have heard of the fine work you are doing down here. I sincerely hope that you will succeed in apprehending the persons who are responsible for the most brutal murders of my great and good friends," he added.

"I hope so too, Mr. Wan," Pullman replied. Then he motioned to Grant and the group made their way to a room, where Wan was shown to a seat.

Pullman began by asking Wan when he had left the mission, why he had not gone directly home, and when he had finally returned to New York. Wan replied that he had left Kalorama Road on Monday, checked into the Harris Hotel because he was feeling ill, and finally departed Washington on the 8:15 p.m. train on Wednesday after having dinner with Ben Sen Wu.

But Pullman was lying in wait for of him.

"Now, Mr. Wan," he scolded, "you have come here, according to your own statement, to help us in this investigation; yet you have started out by telling us two deliberate falsehoods. You did not leave on the 8:15 train and you did not have dinner with Mr. Wu."

He explained that a man answering Wan's description had been seen at the Harris Hotel on Thursday and that the police knew that Wu had eaten with other friends on Wednesday night. Wan replied quickly that whoever had sighted him at the hotel had been mistaken and clarified that Wu had accompanied him to the station and watched him eat some fruit but had not actually *dined* with him on Wednesday.

Then Grant took over, wasting no time with niceties. He sat directly opposite Wan, wagged a finger in his face, and flatly accused him of murder. He also charged him with trying to cash a forged check. Wan, of course, denied everything. At that point, a parade of men entered the room and Wan was ordered to stand, turn around, take off his glasses, and talk with them. These were employees of the Riggs

National Bank, who had already visited the morgue and ruled out all three of the victims as the man who had attempted to cash the check.

"That man there is not the one who presented the check at the bank," George O. Vass, assistant cashier, stated categorically. None of the others could identify Wan either, of course, because he had never been to the bank and none of them had ever seen him before.

Wan was quickly realizing what he had walked into. It was nearing midnight and he was hungry, ill, unhappy, and uncomfortable. Plus, he was being treated anything but courteously. He said he wanted to return to New York. But that was not an option he would be permitted.

In fact, he would not see New York again for seven full years.

4

Incommunicado

ALTHOUGH THE POLICE were not about to permit Wan to leave town, they did offer to take him to a hospital. But he balked at the idea. So Detective Grant decided to bring him to a local hotel instead. Finally, near midnight, without being observed, they checked their exhausted detainee into a room on the second floor of the Dewey Hotel.

The five-story, 140-room Dewey stood at the southeast corner of 14th and L Streets NW. It had recently been renovated and rooms cost $2.00 a night and up. Wan, of course, did not have to pay for his accommodations; the police department took care of that. But they also took care not to register the room in his name. They intended to keep him incommunicado for as long as they interrogated him; this way no one—not reporters nor voyeurs but also not any of his friends nor any attorneys—could find out where he was.

Grant gave orders that Wan was not to leave the room; officers were posted around the clock in eight-hour shifts to enforce this. Nor was he permitted visitors, save the detectives involved in his interrogation. He was allowed newspapers but only after all accounts of the murder case had been excised from them, a procedure that more or less decimated the front pages of the city's broadsheets, which were running headlines like "Hired Assassin Killed Chinese: Police Theory," "Z. S. Wan Stoutly Denies Knowledge of Triple Murder," and "Chinaman's Check a Forgery."[1]

Washington was transfixed with news about the murders. In the absence of concrete information from the interrogation, the newspapers speculated as to what had happened and why, based on what facts were available or, in some cases, rumors that they *thought* were facts. Some of the theories spun were plausible deductions from what was known; others were bizarre, having more to do with racism and popular myths and stereotypes about Asians and their customs than anything else.

The reporters were initially divided on whether robbery had been the motive; they knew Dr. Wong's pockets had not been rifled but there were the earlier reports of petty theft at the mission and a rumor that large sums had been kept in the safe there. They also differed on the order of the murders: some insisted Dr. Wong had been killed first, while others pointed to the fact that Wu was found in his slippers, suggesting that he had been the earliest to return home and the first to die.

Misunderstanding of the Chinese fueled other sorts of speculation. One popular explanation was that the killings had been the work of the Chinese tongs. This would have struck many American readers as plausible, because triad men in Chinatowns across the nation had been killing one another with hatchets and guns for years in a struggle for control of gambling and other vices—Washington's tiny Chinatown was no exception. The journalists were perhaps to be forgiven for failing to realize that Dr. Wong and the other men were not of the ilk to have had truck with Chinatown gangs. But two newspapers stupidly suggested that since the mission was distributing Boxer indemnity funds, Wong's death may have been the work of "Boxer agents." Both were blissfully unaware that the Boxer Rebellion had been suppressed two decades earlier and that Boxers no longer threatened anyone in China or elsewhere.[2]

The *Washington Herald* reported that the "the keenest minds of the Capital's crime detective agencies" had settled on three theories of the crime. First, that Wan was the killer; second, that it had been an insane man *resembling* him; and third, that "agents of a powerful Oriental who is feared by Chinese and Japanese in every quarter of the globe may have committed the crime in the thought that they were halting propaganda activities."

"For years," the *Herald* explained, "it has been gossip among diplomats that one of the most powerful factors in the political life of Japan was a mysterious figure, controlling untold wealth, and known by the title of Toyama." It continued:

FIG. 8. The Dewey Hotel, 1916. Courtesy of the John DeFerrari Collection.

Toyama has been the target for years of many men and many factors. Who he is no one knows. But it is known that his agents are
throughout the world; that they do his bidding without question;
that in many cases they end their own lives with the completion
of the deed to which they are assigned; and that Toyama has often
interfered with the affairs of state and threatened the death of high
officials if they did not promote the imperialistic aims which he
is said to father.[3]

Toyama was not a title, however; it was the name of an actual
person. Mitsuru Toyama was a right-wing Japanese politician who
helped found a terrorist organization and was a strong supporter of
the Japanese occupation of Manchuria. The *Herald* noted that Chen
Ting Wong (Wang Zhengting), a high-ranking Chinese government
official, had passed through Washington recently on his way to the
Paris Peace Conference, where the Chinese government was reso-
lutely opposing Japan's expansionist ambitions in China. Noting the
similarity between the names C. T. Wong and T. T. Wong, it theo-

rized that the assassinations might have been an unfortunate case of mistaken identity on the part of Toyama's agents.[4]

Thorough investigation of the crime scene strongly suggested all three victims had been attacked in the basement, though not necessarily at the same time. Police thought the two younger men had probably been killed there first. Dr. Wong, they believed, had been shot at the foot of the basement stairwell; this would account for the fact that his handkerchief had been found there. His broken spectacles, discovered on the steps, indicated he had tried to flee up the stairs. It was when he got to the reception room on the first floor that he was thought to have been clubbed with the brass lamp as he struggled with his assailant and was shot for the second time. At that point he had dropped to the floor, dead.

By this time the police were fairly certain the $5,000 check brought to Riggs Bank the previous Thursday had been a forgery and that it was very likely related to the murders. They now suspected money *had* been the motive. Major Pullman had examined the mission's checkbook and noticed that whoever had written the draft had also filled in the stub, noting that it had been made out to Dr. Wong himself. This did not square with the memory of the bank employees, who recalled clearly that the check itself had been made payable to "bearer." Nor did the handwriting on the stub look anything like Wong's writing in the rest of the checkbook. Furthermore, a blot of ink on the page from which the check was torn suggested the work of someone very hurried or nervous; the earlier pages in the ledger were uniformly neat.

When the Riggs men failed to finger Wan as the check casher, assistant cashier George O. Vass had remarked that the man who had brought the check had appeared somewhat shorter and younger than Wan. That gave Detective Burlingame the idea that it might have been Wan's brother Van, who fit the bill. So on Sunday, he sent Detective Kelly back to New York to retrieve him. Kelly arrived at Van's room early Monday morning.

Because the police did not have sufficient grounds to arrest Van and knew he was under no obligation to return to Washington with them— although *he* likely did not know this—Kelly resorted to subterfuge to get him to come. He told him his brother was ill and wanted Van to nurse him—that much was true—but omitted the fact that the police had no intention of reuniting the siblings once Van reached the capital.

Van consented. On the train, Kelly casually asked him whether it was a Chinese custom to cover the face of a corpse. He was trying to confirm Burlingame's presumption that that detail of the case pointed to a Chinese murderer. Whether Van suspected his motive is unclear but he replied that he did not think so, because when his other brother had died, no such convention had been observed.

It was dark when they arrived. Burlingame met them at the station and they went by car to 409 Fifteenth Street NW—the same clinic to which Van's brother had been taken two days earlier. Pullman and Grant were there; Grant took over the questioning. As was his practice, he did not mince words. He demanded to know *how* Van had killed the three men. He accused him of being a tong member and peppered him with questions in that vein in a total fishing expedition that led nowhere.

Van, who had not yet eaten that day, asked for food and demanded to see his brother; as he recalled it, he was told he would be allowed to eat and sleep and to see Wan only after he confessed to the murders. He also claimed later that during the interrogation he was cursed, pinched, and shoved. And he recalled an aside by Detective Grant to the effect that, because of the importance of the murdered men, the Chinese Legation was putting tremendous pressure on the police department to solve the case so that they "must get somebody."[5]

The incessant questions continued throughout the night. Finally, shortly before daybreak, Van too was taken to the Dewey, quartered in the room directly above that of his brother, and permitted to sleep. But the two were not allowed to meet. In fact, neither he nor his sibling was told of the other's presence in the hotel.

Also on Sunday, Helen Wong, Dr. Wong's eldest daughter, arrived in Washington. The twenty-year-old, told only that her father was seriously ill, had been summoned by the Chinese Legation from Ann Arbor, Michigan, where she was studying at the university. When upon her arrival she learned of his death and of the circumstances surrounding it, she was distraught. Helen later put to rest rumors that had surfaced in the press that Wan was somehow kin to her family. "He certainly is not related to us in any way," she said, adding, "I have no reason to believe that my father had any enemy."[6]

New evidence trickled in. Police investigators visited the Harris Hotel and interviewed the clerk and a bellhop. The latter recalled the telegrams Wan had sent to his brother; he had run the messages to Western Union himself the previous Monday and Tuesday. The telegraph office confirmed that the wires had been sent to Van in New York and were appeals summoning him to Washington. The front desk clerk remembered Wan checking out on Thursday morning; he recalled this clearly because he had attempted to charge him extra for the second occupant but dropped the issue after Wan had explained that the man was his nurse.

On Monday, the police set about trying to confirm that that "nurse" had been none other than Van and that it had also been he who had gone to Riggs Bank. They postulated that whoever had presented the bogus check would probably have wanted to make a quick getaway, so they began questioning cabbies to determine if any happened to have picked up a Chinese man at Riggs Bank the previous Thursday morning. They found one, a driver for the Terminal Taxicab Company, who recalled the incident clearly. He had in fact taken *two* Chinese *to* the bank that morning and been asked to wait. One had remained in the taxi and the other had gone into the bank with a small suitcase, emerging about a half hour later. Then he had driven them both back to Union Station.

Detectives brought the elevator operator from the Harris, the taxi driver, and the Riggs Bank officers to the Dewey, where all fingered Van. The driver also identified Wan, one floor below, as the man who had stayed in the cab. Although Van denied everything, the police were now certain it had been he who had presented the check. But they could find no trace of it. Detective Kelly had made a third trip to the brothers' New York apartment and rifled through the trunks and bureaus in the room—again, without a warrant—returning with a satchel full of their personal effects and papers. He retrieved the telegrams Wan had sent to summon Van to Washington but the check was nowhere to be found.[7]

By this time, the newspapers had decided that the two brothers were not upstanding men. The *Times* called both of them "'dandies'— the sort who frequent club rooms, play billiards, borrow money from their friends and while they toil not . . . are attired like the proverbial lilies." And both were known to have been in need of money.[8]

The coroner narrowed the probable hour of the murders to some time after 10:30 p.m. on Wednesday, January 29. He noted that cuts found on Dr. Wong's head and right hand suggested that he alone had put up a fight before he died; no such marks appeared on the bodies of the others. And on Monday, he swore in a jury—the practice at the time was for civilians to assist in determining the cause of death—although he did not immediately set a date for an inquest. With the autopsy complete, the bodies were released to Joseph Gawler's Sons, Pennsylvania Avenue undertakers. The Chinese Legation, together with Helen Wong, began arrangements for a triple funeral.[9]

Like Van, Wan stuck to his story, even though parts of it did not add up. There was the discrepancy about when he had actually left Washington, for example. Not only did the staff at the Harris remember seeing him on the morning after the murder was believed to have taken place; the police also had his signature in the hotel register. But other factors pointed elsewhere. A report in the *Washington Herald* suggested that the police believed the crime had to have been committed by someone who had spent time at the mission and knew the routines for issuing checks; this suggested an insider with more knowledge than Wan would likely have gained in his few days as a guest there, and an infirm one at that. Then too, if he *were* guilty, they thought, he likely would have tried to hide rather than return to his known place of residence.

The *Herald* concluded that if more evidence did not materialize soon, the case would probably remain unsolved. "Unless further arrests are made within a short time or new facts developed," it warned, "it is thought his friends will seek by a *habeas corpus* proceeding to force the police either to make charges against Wan or release him."[10]

By Tuesday, February 4, the newspapers were beginning to put two and two together, though not necessarily to total four. They concluded that the check forger must have been the killer. "He wrote the check and filled in the stub while his hands were still trembling from the heinous and wholesale crime he had committed," wrote the *Washington Times*, melodramatically. But they also knew Wan's brother was in their grasp of the police, who suspected he had had a hand in the crime as well but refused to confirm that he was the man who had tried to cash the check.[11]

The papers were beginning to wonder where Wan was. The *Washington Post* complained that police were keeping the young man's whereabouts secret. The press corps had figured out that Major Pullman was his chief interrogator but their many attempts to follow the chief when he left police headquarters were foiled because he could easily shake them by exceeding the speed limit—one of the perquisites of his office. One particularly enterprising reporter hid himself under a blanket in the open back seat of Pullman's car but managed to secure not a scoop, but rather a frigid ride to Pullman's home.[12]

Asked why the men had not been arrested, Major Pullman told a reporter that they were "voluntarily aiding us." But apart from that the detectives had been warned not to discuss the case with the press, though a number of details leaked out anyway. The *Times* somehow found out that Wan "constantly took refuge behind his imperfect knowledge of the English language and American customs" during the questioning. It also noted that although Pullman supposedly did not approve of "third degree methods"—he had been quoted in his first year as chief of police as insisting that better information could be gotten by treating prisoners kindly—Wan had nonetheless been questioned for many hours at a stretch since his arrival on Saturday.

Although there was no reason to believe any physical coercion had taken place, the newspaper suggested that the police had other methods at their disposal.

The *Times* could not have been more right.[13]

5

Interrogation

THE NEWSPAPERS EVENTUALLY figured out Wan's location but, at the request of the authorities, did not publish the name of the hotel. The police wanted the freedom to examine Wan without interruption, the *Washington Times* explained. And by midweek, the detectives had begun to feel confident that they were within reach of solving the case, despite the fact that the evidence was still largely circumstantial.[1]

They knew Wan had been at the scene of the crime within a few hours of the time it was committed, that he and his brother were in need of money, and that Van had attempted to cash the forged check. Under unrelenting pressure, Wan admitted that he had not left town until the day *after* the murder—something they already knew—but he had said no more than that. Since they had not secured a confession, however, they needed more proof before they would be in a position to file formal charges.[2]

One additional piece of evidence that had come to light was a $50 check Ben Sen Wu had written to Wan on January 13 that had been cashed a week later. Like his signature in the Harris Hotel guest book, Wan's endorsement on the back of Wu's check appeared similar to the writing on the stub of the $5,000 check in the mission's register. This potentially linked Wan to the forgery; it was also further testimony to a close relationship between Wan and Wu and to the fact that there was a debt between the two men.

On Wednesday, funeral services were held for the three murdered men at St. Andrew's Episcopal Church at New Hampshire Avenue and V Street NW, where both Dr. Wong and Hsie had been congregants. Helen Wong, Kang Li, and Chinese Legation staff were among the mourners. When the simple service was over, the bodies were taken to Rock Creek Cemetery and placed in a temporary vault, pending removal to China.[3]

As the week wore on, the incessant interrogations at the Dewey Hotel continued. Wan asked repeatedly for his brother but his keepers did not even admit that Van was in Washington until Thursday. Even then they did not permit the brothers to meet, Pullman explained, because "we knew if these boys once began talking Chinese to one another our investigation of the case might end right there."[4] The men were questioned separately and repeatedly at odd hours of the day, sometimes quite late into the night. Pullman visited every day and Burlingame, Grant, and Kelly took turns quizzing both detainees. Even when Wan got tired or irritated and asked to be left alone, the ceaseless cross-examination continued. At such times, Detective Kelly recalled, "sometimes we did and sometimes we did not let him alone." On occasion Wan just remained silent, refusing to speak for a half hour at a time.[5]

At times the detectives were warm and solicitous. Burlingame had promised Wan in New York that he would be treated well in Washington; apart from keeping him incarcerated against his will and bombarding him with incessant questions, he did attempt to make good on that pledge by making Wan as comfortable as possible under the circumstances. Wan was permitted to order whatever meals he desired, for example, even though he could digest very little. He was provided with cigars if he wanted them. The hotel staff shined his shoes. And he was engaged on many topics that had nothing to do with the crime. Pullman recalled wide-ranging discussions on such topics as international politics, the League of Nations, and Chinese customs and literature, among others.

At other times the questioners were insulting and abusive. Wan recollected that Burlingame often used profanity. Van was more specific: he reported being pointed at and called a yellow rat, a "Chink," a skunk, and other names, and being pinched and pushed. Wan was constantly accused of being a murderer. At one point, he recalled, upon learning that he was a Christian, Major Pullman had handed him a Bible and insisted to him that God wanted him to confess.[6]

There is little doubt that the detectives looked down on their

FIG. 9. *From left*, District of Columbia Police Inspector Clifford L. Grant and Detective Sergeants Edward J. Kelly and Guy E. Burlingame. Source: *Washington Times*.

charges, as many Americans derided Chinese people during that era and saw them as a breed apart. The press coverage, no less racist, suggests the depth of the disdain. The *Times* noted helpfully for its readers that "the Oriental is known among judges and lawyers as the most difficult person to examine. His wheaten countenance does not change color with accompanying emotions as does the Caucasian, and long generations of stoical ancestors have given him an imperturbability which almost defies ruffling." And the Washington *Evening Star* assured its readers by quoting "unnamed criminologists" as stating categorically that "Chinese never confess."[7]

The prejudice of the police was evident throughout the process. But the bigotry may have had far more serious ramifications than the humiliation engendered by an occasional racist epithet. The authorities clearly took advantage of the fact that the men were foreigners, unschooled in the American legal system, even though they were still entitled to equal protection of the laws and to due process.[8] The brothers probably did not know, for example, that they had not been obliged to accompany the detectives back to Washington; they could have refused and forced the District of Columbia to seek their extradition. They may not have been aware that they were entitled to legal counsel and could have requested it at any time. The detectives were not obliged to advise them of their rights or to inform them that anything they said could be used against them in court—they made no effort to do so. And the brothers certainly were not cognizant of the option to seek a writ of habeas corpus to end the interminable interrogation, or there is little doubt they would have pursued it.[9]

Throughout the week Wan suffered terribly, still experiencing severe symptoms of the influenza he had contracted the previous year, made all the worse by the relentless pressure. He complained of discomfort in his abdomen and could digest little of his food, sometimes vomiting shortly after eating. He experienced constant constipation and remained unable to move his bowels unless assisted by an enema. And he was weak overall, spending most of his time in bed. He asked repeatedly for a doctor. The detectives did arrange several visits by a police surgeon, a general practitioner. But the doctor was able to do little to relieve his suffering. His chief contribution seems to have been to assure the officers that Wan was "in no immediate danger of death."[10]

Yet pain or no pain, the ceaseless questions continued.

Both men consistently denied any knowledge of the forged check. But on Friday afternoon, while Inspector Grant was interviewing Van in his room at the Dewey on his fifth day in detention, he asked matter-of-factly what Van had thought when he received the telegrams summoning him to Washington. Van answered that he had believed he was going to be offered a job.

Suddenly, however, his eyes welled up, and he blurted out the words, "They fool me!" In other words, he felt he had been set up. He then acknowledged that it had indeed been he who had gone to the bank, which of course the detectives already knew from the bank employees. But it was the first time he had confessed it. Armed with this admission, Grant rushed downstairs, where Burlingame and Kelly were questioning Wan. He intended to use the information to entrap Wan.[11]

"Now Wan, the check is a separate proposition, and it has nothing to do with the murder. Just leave the murder out of it; tell me who went to the bank and attempted to get the check cashed," Grant exhorted. "Go ahead, Wan, and tell me who went to the bank."

"If you find the man who went to the bank with the check, you will have found the murderer," Wan replied.

"Well, we *know* who went to the bank with the check. Your brother

FIG. 10. Tsong Ing Van, ca. 1915. Source: National Archives and Records Administration.

Van went into the bank, and he has told us about it," Grant revealed. "He told us that he went into the bank with a check and attempted to get it cashed, and he left you outside."

"It is a lie; it is a lie; my brother tell you nothing," Wan exclaimed, agitated. He jumped up and down, enraged, and pounded the bed. And then he pulled the bedclothes over himself and would say no more.[12]

Sensing an opportunity, the police decided the time had come to permit the brothers to meet. They made elaborate preparations for the rendezvous, which was to take place the next day at the mission on Kalorama Road. They thought that forcing Wan to relive the night of the murder at the crime scene might finally elicit a confession, or at very least that watching his reactions might give them further insights. They were also intensely interested in anything he and his brother might have to say to each other. The plan they hatched was for the brothers to be taken to the mission separately, Wan first and Van later, and for Kang Li, the young man who had discovered the dead men and who was apparently no longer a suspect in their murder, to hide in the second-floor sitting room closet so he might overhear and report on anything they said to each other in Chinese.

The police were finished with cigars and shoe shines. They were ready to play hardball.

Just after 7:00 p.m. on Saturday, February 8, the detectives bundled Wan up and took him, under cover of darkness, to the mission. Wan said later that he was in such pain at the time that he "could not stand straight."[13] There they were joined by Major Pullman. When they arrived, Wan peppered the police with questions, asking exactly where the bodies and the revolver had been found. In the first-floor reception room, he was told that a crimson stain on the floor was the blood of Dr. Wong. He stared at the spot for a full five minutes, Burlingame recalled, then asked about the position of the body. Shown one of the crime scene photographs of the corpse, he sighed, "So sorry; so sorry." He had a similar reaction when they descended into the basement, where the other bodies had been discovered in the furnace room, but overall seemed "very cold and calm," according to Detective Kelly.

It was on the second floor that the brothers met for the first time since Wan's hasty departure from New York a week earlier. When Van arrived, Wan jumped up and pumped his hand.

"How are you?" Wan asked, in English.

"Fine, fine. How are you?" his brother responded.

"Just my stomach, my stomach," he said. But to the detectives' disappointment, nothing of substance was said in Chinese.

Somehow the press found out about the meeting, probably because they were watching the hotel. Reporters massed outside the town-house and began ringing the doorbell. They also telephoned the mission repeatedly and honked their horns, forcing the officers to take Wan and Van up to the third floor, where it was quieter and there was no possibility of being overheard by a zealous newsman.[14]

There, in the company of Grant, Kelly, and a stenographer, Pullman confronted Wan with Dr. Wong's checkbook and with samples of his own signature. Noting the similarities between Wan's writing and that on the check stub, he asked him to compare the specimens himself and demanded to know whose writing was on the stub.

"I think I write that," Wan admitted, after a long pause.

"We do not want to know what you *think*," Pullman admonished him. "We want the truth and all the information that you and your brother can give us."

"Yes, I wrote it," Wan conceded.[15]

The grilling, sometimes civil and sometimes rude, continued.

Both brothers later recounted that both Burlingame and Kelly had cursed them and spewed racial epithets at them that night. Van recalled them being called "yellow rats" and "skunks." But Pullman, who did not use profanity, was more strategic. The detectives had come to understand that Van was Wan's weakness; he had constantly asked for his brother since he had been brought down from New York and his consternation upon being told that Van had confessed to attempting to cash the check was telling. It was clear to them that Wan cared a great deal for his brother and did not want to see him implicated.

Pullman wagged his finger in Wan's face and declared, "He is as cold-blooded a Chinaman as I ever saw. Why don't you admit and let your brother go? You say you are a good Christian and love your brother. Why don't you *admit*?"

When this approach failed, Grant tried to bait Wan by suggesting that it had been a case of self-defense and that nobody was to blame.

"Just answer yes and we will all go and get something warm to eat and then we will go to bed," he said. "They were three and you were one and surely you could not kill them three because you are in a weak condition and the pistol is Wu's. Surely they tried to strike you and then you grabbed the pistol from Wu and shot them three; everybody will believe that," he coaxed.

Failing again to elicit the desired reaction from Wan, Grant then suggested that perhaps Wu had killed the other two and then Wan had grabbed the pistol and shot him before he could kill him too.[16] Then Kelly piled on with more pointed questions, at which point Wan grew silent.

"Why don't you answer Mr. Kelly? Why don't you tell him what he asked you?" Burlingame demanded.

Wan then said something to his brother in Chinese.

"Stop that," Burlingame commanded. "If you are going to talk to Van, talk in English." At which point the exasperated Chinese man picked up a coat hanger and attempted to strike the detective with it.

"Stop that," Burlingame ordered again, grabbing his ailing captive by his shoulders and shoving him back into his chair. "We don't want anything like that and we will not have it."[17]

Wan regained his composure and apologized for losing his temper, though if the circumstances of the interrogation were anything like the brothers recalled, his reaction was understandable. "We won't let you alone until you admit how you killed them," Grant had threatened, Van recalled. Grant even poked the ailing Wan with the murder weapon. Van asked for water and a trip to the toilet, both of which were refused. No food was offered. After Burlingame pushed Wan into the chair, he had slumped onto the floor; when Van handed him a cushion for support, he recalled, Detective Kelly snatched it away and warned, "Don't think you are home. You are in our power. You have got to do what we say."

The detectives were trying to make the brothers as uncomfortable as possible.

Apart from his admission about the check, Wan was unwavering on other details and stuck to his story. Major Pullman finally went home at midnight and Detective Grant actually fell asleep on one of the mission's beds. But Wan, exhausted and in excruciating pain, was permitted no sleep; Kelly and Burlingame continued to badger him ceaselessly into the wee hours. It was not until about 5:00 a.m.

that the brothers were allowed to leave. Wan recounted later that he was so drained that the detectives literally had to carry him out of the mission.[18]

Because the press already knew all about the Dewey Hotel, it would have been impossible to return the men there without being observed, but in any case the detectives had decided on a different destination: the Tenth Precinct. Wan had now admitted to forgery and Van to being his accomplice. Even without a confession of murder, these disclosures were enough—finally—to justify formally placing the men under arrest.

The detectives sensed that the denouement was near.

6

Confession

THE STEEL CELLS of the stately Tenth Precinct Station House at 750 Park Road NW had failed to contain Harry Houdini, who famously escaped incarceration there in a 1909 stunt. Stripped naked, the great escape artist had freed himself from a set of handcuffs, defeated the five locks that secured his cell, and opened those of an adjacent chamber that held his clothing—all within the space of eighteen minutes.[1]

A decade later, however, Ziang Sung Wan was far more interested in sleep than escape. He was finally permitted to rest but only until Sunday evening, when Grant, Burlingame, and Kelly returned and resumed their questioning of him in the sergeant's room. Van was not present but the detectives were joined by Kang Sung Wang, a young Shanghainese studying at Columbia University. Detective Kelly had located Wang through Mrs. Bartels, Wan's landlady, and brought him down from New York after the police discovered, from a telegram he had sent, that he was a friend of the brothers. They thought Wan might be more likely to confide in a buddy than confess to a police officer.[2]

Having determined that Wan was most apprehensive about implicating his brother, Inspector Grant decided to hammer away at that theme. "If you are guilty and your brother is innocent, now is the time to tell it; I want to know," Grant demanded, "for I am holding your brother just the same as I am holding you." He added that things looked very bad for Wan, as the police were now certain he knew more about the crime than he had admitted.

"If you did not kill these people, then I want you to tell me who did," Grant enjoined. At that point, Wan conceded that he *had* been present when the three men were killed but would not say more. He asked to speak privately with Kang. The two men began conversing in Chinese while the detectives left the room.[3]

Eventually, they were asked back in and Wan made an admission. He had been in the house when the murders took place, he said, but had not participated in them. He told the police that Ben Sen Wu had shot his two colleagues and that a New York–based Chinese businessman named C. H. Chen had subsequently killed Wu. The officers pressed him for details but he declined to go on without more sleep. He promised to tell more the next day.

By the following morning the newspapers knew all about Wan's admission as well as his acknowledgment that he had forged the check. They had also been briefed on Wan's prediction that "if you find the man who went to the bank with the check, you will have found the murderer." They quoted the police as accepting these declarations "as a virtual confession of participation in the murder."[4]

But a "virtual" confession was not the same as a real one, and there was still far more to the story than the police had been told. Wan asked to be taken back to the mission, explaining that it would be easier to show the detectives what had happened than to tell them about it. Just after 10:00 a.m. they drove him back to Kalorama Road.

Wan explained there that, before he had moved out of the mission the previous Monday, he and Ben Sen Wu had hatched a scheme to steal a check from the mission's checkbook and cash it. Wu alone knew that he had not returned to New York, Wan said, but rather had checked into the Harris Hotel. Wu had visited him there on Tuesday, the day before the murder, to report that he had stolen a blank check. The two men had met again early Wednesday afternoon at the mission to plot their next steps.

But by then, Wan said, Dr. Wong had learned of the theft. Wu believed Hsie had discovered it and alerted him. Wong had called the police, accounting for Detective Bradley's visit to the mission on the day of the murders. Wu had been blamed and was fearful he might be humiliated and lose his job. He told Wan to come back after dinner, so the two of them could fill out the check. Wan went back to his hotel. When evening came he sent Van out to a movie and returned to the mission alone. Wu had left the door open for him.

It was only about fifteen minutes after he arrived that Kang Li had knocked on the door and he had sent him away. But Wu then phoned the mission and announced he would not be back until about 9:00 p.m., so Wan once again returned to his hotel. By the time he got back to the mission a second time, Wu had arrived; he had probably been there when Detective Bradley pushed his business card through the mail slot but had declined to answer the door.

Wu brought Wan upstairs to Hsie's second-floor office and produced the checkbook; Wan, whose English was far better than Wu's, filled out the stub and Wu stamped the date on the check. Then they went downstairs to the kitchen, where Wan filled it out for $5,000 and Wu drafted the letter Van would later take to Riggs Bank. It was while they were discussing who would go to the bank to claim the funds that Chang Hsi Hsie had walked in.

At this point, Inspector Grant interrupted him. "Wan, you know how this happened. I know there was no Chen. *You* are the man that you are placing here in the story as Chen."

Grant then placed his hand on Wan's shoulder and looked him straight in the eye. After a long pause, whether due to the cumulative effects of nine days of unrelenting questions, sleep deprivation, a throbbing bowel, a desire to exonerate his brother, or a guilty conscience, the Chinese man replied softly, "Yes, I will tell you the whole truth now. Chen was not in it."

He had been sitting in the kitchen and Wu standing at the sink when Hsie came in at about 10:30 p.m., he continued. Once Hsie turned his back on Wu, the latter pulled out his pistol and shot at him. Hsie tried to escape into the furnace room but Wu followed him there and Wan heard two more shots. When Wu emerged, he shut the door behind him, reloaded the gun with some shells retrieved from one of the kitchen drawers, and put the gun back in his pocket. Then the two sat silently for a while, except that Wu muttered under his breath that he had always hated Hsie. There was no discussion of the shooting. When the silence was broken, the only talk was a renewal of the conversation about cashing the check.

Less than a half hour later, someone else entered the house. "Here comes old Wong," Wu had whispered. They could hear Dr. Wong take

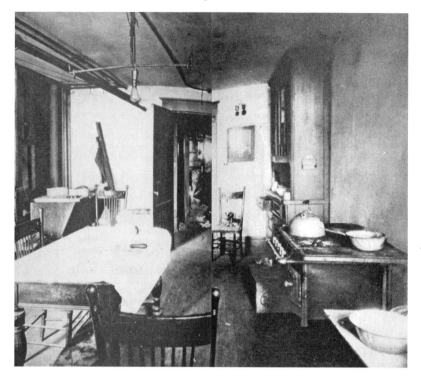

FIG. 11. A view of the basement kitchen at the Chinese Educational Mission.
Source: *Evening Star.*

off his coat, stop briefly in his office, and then mount the stairs to the second floor. It took about ten minutes for him to make his way downstairs to the basement. When he entered the kitchen he seemed surprised to see Wan, whom he believed to have returned to New York. Before he could mouth a greeting, however, Wu drew the revolver and shot him point blank in the chest, Wan recalled. Wong turned and rushed back up the stairs, dropping his spectacles. Wu followed; Wan did not. But shortly afterward, Wan heard something break and the sound of one or two more shots, then silence. He didn't move.

It took Wu a while to reappear downstairs; when he did, he had changed his clothes. Wan was frightened and very upset at the murder of Dr. Wong, whom he had known all his life. He did not let on how he felt but in that moment, he told the detectives, he resolved to kill Wu. Wu laid the revolver on the kitchen table, without speaking, and motioned to Wan to come and sit near him. Then he told Wan—by way of rehearsing him—that *both* of them had killed Wong and Hsie.

Wan protested that *he* had not killed anyone. The two continued to disagree about who should present the check at the bank and then about whether they should remain at the mission that night. Wu wanted Wan to stay but Wan, who was superstitious, was uncomfortable sleeping under the same roof as two corpses. Besides, the house was quite cold.

Wan got up and paced about the room, eventually going to the drawer and surreptitiously fetching some bullets. He let a little time go by, then picked up the gun and silently loaded the shells. He said he did not think Wu noticed. Then he suggested they put some coal in the furnace and followed Wu into the furnace room, carrying the pistol. It was there that he fired at Wu, who fell face down, almost on top of Hsie. Wan told the police that he then rolled him over and shot him a second time.

Wan left the gun on a chair. After washing blood off his hands in the kitchen sink, he turned off the light and went upstairs. He cried at the sight of Dr. Wong's body, he recalled, before leaving the building. He then rendezvoused with his brother near the Garden Theatre on Ninth Street NW. He did not tell Van all that had happened, he insisted, although he later admitted to telling him he had shot Wu.

"My brother is absolutely innocent," Wan explained. "He had no part in the killing. He knew nothing of it. He was only my tool in attempting to pass the forged check." And the next day, after the bank refused to cash the draft, the brothers had returned to New York. It was in the toilet of the northbound train that Wan had disposed of it.[5]

Immediately following Wan's confession, he was accused of murder and formally arrested. Van was not arrested but the detectives said he would shortly be charged as an accomplice after the fact.

The evening edition of the *Washington Times* proclaimed that the "internationally famous triple Chinese murder mystery which has been agitating two continents" had been solved. The paper's lead story, it appeared under a three-line, seven-column banner headline. Portraits of Pullman, Grant, Kelly, and Burlingame on page two were captioned, "The men who solved the Chinese mystery and forced the guilty to confess." The newspaper even ran a signed article by Major Pullman in which he took a public victory lap.

The police chief likened the lengthy interrogation to "working low content gold ore," crowing that "we had to labor hard and spend a great deal of time to get the small but important connecting facts in the story." He congratulated himself and his detectives and thanked the law-abiding Chinese, the citizens of Washington, and the newspapers for their cooperation.[6]

Pullman was confident Wan had finally told the truth. He pointed out that the Chinese man had nothing to gain by implicating Wu, because "he is just as bad off with a confession of one murder against him as he would be with three." And the police had learned from others that there had indeed been animosity between Wu and Hsie, giving further credence to the notion that Wu had played a role in the killings.

Back at the Tenth Precinct, the brothers shared a cell, where Van doted on his elder sibling. He made his bed, propped his head up on pillows, and did what he could to make Wan comfortable. "The solicitude was touching," the *Times* wrote, "and made it easy for the police to understand how completely under Wan's dominance Van had been when told to go to the bank and cash the bogus check."[7]

There was still the matter of a written confession. With a stenographer present, Burlingame told Wan that the police wished him to make a statement but that he was under no obligation to do so. He also informed him that it could be used against him in court—the first time, as far as is known, that this was said. Wan sat on the edge of the bed and suggested that Burlingame use a question-and-answer format. The statement, once typed, ran for twenty-one pages; Wan was asked to affix his signature and initials to each page. He later recalled that when he finally signed it, he was in "an almost dying condition."[8]

"The police have a perfect prima facie case against Wan and Van," U.S. attorney for the District of Columbia John E. Laskey told the *Washington Herald* later that day. A well-regarded jurist, Laskey had been in the job since 1914 and had been reappointed in 1918 by President Woodrow Wilson for what the *Washington Post* described as his ability, diligence, and tact. He added that there was "more than ample evidence to assure the Grand Jury holding them to trial on a first degree murder charge."[9]

But first there was the matter of the inquest. As was the practice in the early twentieth century, the coroner swore in a six-member jury on Monday, February 10, to assist him in determining the cause of death. The following day Wan appeared before them. But Wan's confession had been so detailed, and it was so clear that the deaths would be ruled murders, that only a few of the principal witnesses in the case were presented to the jury. Before it had even rendered its verdict, cells were being prepared for the brothers at the District of Columbia jail.

"I'm glad this is off of my mind," Wan told Inspector Grant. "Dr. Wong was my friend and my mother in Shanghai had entrusted him to care for me in this country. I never wanted him killed, so I killed Wu for what he had done. I am glad it is all over." He added, "You now have the whole truth. I am not going to fight the case you have built up against me. I want no lawyer. I know what I have done, and I will 'take my medicine,' as you Americans say."[10]

On Tuesday, after hearing testimony from representatives of the police and Riggs Bank and from Kang Li, the coroner's jury was ready to complete its inquest. But first, both men, neither of whom was represented by counsel, were asked if they wished to make statements. Both did, even after a warning from the coroner that they could be used against them. Van, who was biting his fingernails and clearly very nervous, spoke first. "I only want to say that I knew nothing about the check," he said. "I got it in an envelope and when I went into the bank I passed over the envelope with the check in it."

By contrast, Wan evinced no anxiety when he took the stand. "I got a telegram last December from Wu asking me to come on a visit to Washington. I was sick then and could not come. Last month I came here and went to the Mission. Dr. Wong wanted me to stay. Wu was afraid that Dr. Wong was going to transfer him to some other place. Van had nothing to do with the murders." Then he added—contradicting his earlier signed statement—"I do not know anything about the check. Wu arranged that. That's all I can say."

The coroner's jury, of course, ruled that the deaths had been murders. Despite Wan's confession and statements by the police that *they* believed Van had played no part in the killings, the members found *both* men responsible for all three deaths. Van's indictment was a shock. It persuaded Wan of the wisdom of obtaining counsel.

"I must have a lawyer now," he said, "because they do not believe what I tell them. I have told them the truth that my brother might not suffer. Now they are going to punish him, too. I must make them understand that I am the only man living who is to blame."[11]

But the brothers could not afford legal counsel. Wan had not worked for quite a while, and his bank account still stood at $41.07. Van had been employed for a time in Providence, but he had likely been supporting his brother. Nor was the Chinese Legation in any mood to help them. "If these boys have broken the laws of this country, they must pay the penalty. We can only commend them to the justice and mercy of an American jury," said Chargé d'Affaires Yung Kwai. Whether the legation could not, or *would* not, lift a finger to help the young men is unclear. The victims, after all, had been their colleagues and friends.

"If no friends rally to their support, the judge before whom they are arraigned will assign an attorney," the *Times* assured its readers. In the meantime the brothers were transferred to the District jail, where they were held for action of the grand jury.[12]

It would be Wan's home for far longer than anyone could imagine.

7

Indictment and Trial

ABOUT 300 PRISONERS were in residence in the District jail when Wan and Van arrived, though the population was quite fluid. Nearly 6,000 people passed through its doors that year, but most were soon discharged or transferred. The majority were black; eighty-five percent were male. Nearly a third had been locked up for intoxication but the range of offenses included assault, disorderly conduct, carrying a deadly weapon, vagrancy, forgery, fornication, breaking and entering, larceny, robbery, and nonsupport. Forty-eight of the inmates had been accused or convicted of murder.[1]

A large, four-story stone building located on 19th Street SE, the jail had been built in 1875. It had been fitted out with 300 cells, each five by eight feet, but without proper plumbing facilities. Although forty eight more cubicles were added and modern plumbing was finally installed, by the early twentieth century the jailhouse was criticized by President William Howard Taft as "antiquated and unsanitary."[2]

The jail was also where executions were carried out. Until electrocution was introduced in 1926, those convicted of first-degree murder were hanged; when Wan and Van arrived a gallows still stood inside the building, visible from many of the cells. Erected of oak timber in 1882 for the hanging of the convicted assassin of President James A. Garfield, it had ended the lives of fifty men by 1919. By year's end it would be moved to a nearby building, but when the brothers arrived, the scaffold's looming presence served as a constant and daunting reminder of what lay in store for them should they be convicted.[3]

The men were permitted to share a cell so that Van might minister to his ailing brother, whose dyspepsia had worsened since the confession. They were assigned to a hall known colloquially as "murderers' row" with others awaiting trial on capital murder charges.[4]

The day after they arrived, Wan experienced such a serious gastric attack that Dr. James A. Gannon, the jail's chief medical officer, was summoned. His diagnosis was colitis. Although Wan's condition was not judged critical, he was sufficiently ill to have to be carried to the jail's Red Cross room. It was there, in severe pain, that he finally signed the confession the police had typed up.[5]

Wan let the warden know that he and Van had been baptized in China and asked for a meeting with an Episcopal priest. Major Pullman personally brought the Reverend J. Henning Nelms, pastor of the Church of the Ascension, to visit the brothers on February 13. There was no discussion of the case during the half-hour meeting; the four men merely prayed together.[6]

Over the next several days Wan met with a lawyer and U.S. Attorney John E. Laskey began to prepare his case for the grand jury. Inspector Grant turned over Wan's confession and lists of witnesses and exhibits; the latter included Wu's pistol, several shells, and the suitcase Van had taken to Riggs Bank, as well as garments found on the dead men. Laskey took a deep interest in the case. He visited the Kalorama Road house, conducted a thorough examination of the premises, and had several pictures of the crime scene taken.[7]

It took four full months before Laskey presented the case to a grand jury and another three for the body to complete its deliberations. Despite his comment in February about having "more than ample evidence" to support a charge of first-degree murder, Laskey in fact found, after reviewing the record and the evidence, much fault with the work of the police. He felt, the *Washington Post* reported, that he had no choice but to delay asking for indictments.

First there was the matter of the confession, which Wan had already repudiated. Because of the circumstances under which it had been obtained, Laskey believed it would be risky to go to court with *only* that apart from the circumstantial evidence. The *Post* suggested presciently that it "might not be worth the paper it is printed on." Second, Laskey believed the police had overlooked some potentially important leads. For example, Wan had been seen at the Harris Hotel on

FIG. 12. Interior view of a cell block in the District of Columbia Jail, 1919.
Source: Library of Congress, LC-H261-30606.

the night of the murder in the company of a tall Chinese man not his brother but the police had not investigated who he might have been.[8]

Laskey eventually did go forward, however. And at the end of September, after hearing testimony from seventeen witnesses, including Detectives Grant and Kelly, three employees of Riggs Bank, the elevator operator and night clerk at the Harris Hotel, two Chinese diplomats, and two Chinese students, the grand jury did indeed hand down indictments—four of them, in all.

Three of the four were against Wan, who was accused of all three murders. If there was any good news, it was for Van. Unlike the coroner's jury, the grand jury accepted that he had not been a party to murder. But they believed he knew more about his trip to the bank than he had let on and charged him with passing a forged check.[9]

On October 7 both brothers pleaded not guilty before Judge Ashley M. Gould, a former U.S. attorney who had been appointed to the Supreme Court of the District of Columbia in 1902 by President Theodore Roosevelt.[10] They were represented by forty-one-year-old James

A. O'Shea and his partner, John I. Sacks, as well as twenty-seven-year-old Charles Fahy, a Georgetown Law School graduate and former World War I navy aviator. Wan was, of course, held without bail because he was accused of murder. Laskey asked for bond of $5,000 for Van but the judge reduced the amount to $3,000.[11] Two days later, Van's bail was posted by a William W. Stewart, whose relationship to the brothers is unknown; Van then left for home in New York City.

The press, in general, was not on Wan's side. But on the eve of the trial, he was the beneficiary of some surprisingly sympathetic coverage in the *Washington Times* that foreshadowed the strategy of the defense:

> If you can picture an American boy, slightly over twenty, 6,000 miles away from home, being tried for murder in a Chinese court, before a Chinese judge and a Chinese jury, according to Chinese law and customs, you can imagine something of the predicament of young Ziang Sung Wan . . .
>
> The police say young Wan has confessed. They have a typewritten document to which the boy's signature is attached. Wan has now repudiated this recital of one of the most extraordinary slaying mysteries in American criminal records. He declares it was obtained under great duress: that he was the victim of one of the most searching and cruel third degrees to which any suspect was ever subjected; that advantage was taken of his ignorance of American law and that his rights and privileges under the law were violated beyond all right and reason.[12]

On December 9, two months after he entered his plea and ten months to the day since his arrest, Ziang Sung Wan was finally put on trial. Laskey had decided that trying him for the murder of Ben Sen Wu offered the best chance of conviction; it was the only killing to which he had ever confessed and most of the other evidence was circumstantial. Nor were there any eyewitnesses. The first hurdle was swearing in a jury, which proved far more difficult than expected.

One sticking point was the death penalty, the mandatory punishment for first-degree murder. Twenty-three people were excused in the first two days because they opposed capital punishment. Oth-

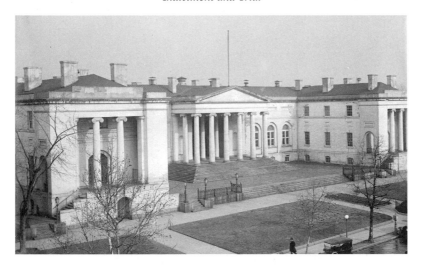

FIG. 13. The Supreme Court of the District of Columbia met in the "Old City Hall" building at Judiciary Square from 1863 to 1926. Source: Library of Congress, LC-H261-2512-A.

ers were let go because they had already formed opinions about the case. But attorney O'Shea made sure that the use of the third degree was also raised in the voir dire process. He asked all potential jurors if they would afford a confession obtained after eight days' grilling of a sick prisoner denied communication with his friends as much consideration as one given voluntarily under different circumstances.

By the third day, eleven jurors had been selected but it took until December 15 to fill the twelfth spot, marking a new record for the court. Jury selection had never before required more than five days. This time nearly 300 people were examined.[13]

A large crowd filed into the Old City Hall building at Judiciary Square on the first day of testimony in the case of the *United States v. Ziang Sung Wan*. The venerable structure, where John H. Surratt had once been tried for conspiracy to assassinate President Abraham Lincoln and Charles Guiteau had been convicted of the murder of President James A. Garfield, had been renovated the previous year. The makeover had included installation of heating in the basement, where Wan, immaculately turned out in a suit and tie, was held each

FIG. 14. Judge Ashley M. Gould's courtroom during the 1919 trial of the *United States v. Ziang Sung Wan*. The defendant can be seen (*second from right in foreground*) seated behind his attorney, James A. O'Shea. Assistant U.S. Attorney Bolitha J. Laws is seated across the aisle from O'Shea. Source: Library of Congress, LC-F82-3409.

day while awaiting his appearance in court. The second and third floors had been newly fitted out with eight courtrooms. One of them was Judge Gould's.[14]

Assistant U.S. Attorney Bolitha J. Laws delivered the opening statement for the People, setting out the chronology of events. But the aptly named Laws, a twenty-eight-year-old Georgetown Law School graduate, tried as best he could to present a case that avoided relying too heavily on Wan's confession because he knew the document was vulnerable to challenge and might be thrown out. Laws needed to make a case that could survive that eventuality; he built it by playing up Wan's financial difficulties and suggesting his need to cover up forgery as the motive for the crime. "It is doubtful if a clearer case of circumstantial evidence was ever placed before a court by a prosecutor in his opening statement concerning a tragedy," the *Washington Post* remarked.[15]

Attorney O'Shea declined to offer an opening statement until the government had presented its case, so the prosecution began to call its witnesses; there were fifty-five in all on its list. Those who took the stand on the first day, mostly from New York, established Wan's financial condition, his illness, and the dates he and his brother had been out of town. O'Shea objected frequently to the proceedings, beginning the accrual of a long list of "exceptions"—that is, objections—that might be cited on appeal.

Dr. Kang Li testified the next day. The prosecution put him on the stand to describe his encounter with Wan on the mission doorstep and his discovery of the bodies, which coincidentally that same day began their final journey from the receiving vault at Rock Creek Cemetery back to permanent rest in Shanghai. The defense used Li's presence very effectively to suggest that he had cooperated with the police in order to deflect suspicion of his own guilt. To portray Li as a credible suspect, O'Shea established that Li himself had been a guest at the mission and that he had, for a time at least, possessed a key to the front door.[16]

The following day, the jury saw photographs of the corpses in situ at the death house and heard from the coroner. They also heard Detective—now Lieutenant—Burlingame describe his trip to New York with Detective Kelly and admit, on cross-examination, that he had *not* told Wan that anything he might say could be used against him in court. O'Shea knew that his best bet for getting the confession suppressed would be to prove that Wan had been pressured into making it, so he hammered away at the circumstances surrounding the interrogation. He would do the same with all the police witnesses.

He questioned Burlingame about where Wan had been sequestered, for how long, and why he had been denied contact with anyone but the police. He asked him whether Wan had been forced to stand during interrogations and whether he had been made to go without food. O'Shea wanted to know what times of day the questioning had taken place, whether profanity had been used, whether Wan had always spoken voluntarily, and how sick he was when he made his statement.

The detective allowed that Wan had once been questioned after midnight but denied he had been forced to stand. He insisted Wan had always been offered food and denied using profane language.

He admitted Wan had given his statement while lying in bed. But "as far as his being sick," Burlingame said, "I told him he was sick in the head more than in the body." Throughout, he steadfastly denied that Wan had been coerced in any way.[17]

Inspector Grant, up next, denied that Wan had been in any way abused, stating that he had always been treated humanely. But he admitted that Wan had not been permitted to see his brother for five days.[18]

"Isn't it true that Wan demanded frequently to be let alone?" O'Shea inquired.

"Yes, he frequently asked to be let alone."

"Did you let him alone?"

"Well, not always," Grant answered. "Wan had a very vicious disposition. He would declare, when asked embarrassing questions, that he would incriminate himself if he answered. We would leave him alone for a while, and then question him again."[19]

To counter the perception that Wan had been starved to weaken his resistance, Laws produced charge slips from the Dewey Hotel. He must have been jubilant when the *Washington Herald* concluded from them that Wan had "lived like a lord" while in police custody. "Food galore if he wanted it, a cigar thrown in if desired, a shoe shine to help keep up his natty appearance and a deck of cards with which to amuse himself, was the usual treatment accorded Ziang Sun Wan [*sic*]," it recounted on December 20.[20]

Because of a juror's illness and the Christmas holiday, the court recessed and the trial did not resume until December 29, when the judge ruled Wan's confession admissible. "If the police went beyond the proprieties," he stated, "the jury would be told that a confession so obtained would not be voluntary. The limits to which the police may go depends [*sic*] on the circumstances of each case. They have a right to use all reasonable methods in getting facts in a case." The ruling, which permitted the jury to draw its own conclusions on the validity of the confession, dealt a severe blow to the defense's case.[21]

The next day it was Major Pullman's turn to testify. He added nothing new and was on the stand for only fifteen minutes. He was followed by Inspector Grant and Detective Kelly, both of whom reinforced the

FIG. 15. Judge Ashley M. Gould, ca. 1911. Courtesy of Margot Bucholtz.

police narrative that Wan had been treated kindly as a "guest of the Washington Police Department" and that he had made many conflicting and incriminating statements during that time.[22]

On December 31 Wan's confession was read aloud to the jury, which up to that point had only heard *about* it. That, together with O'Shea's failure to elicit admission of mistreatment from the police witnesses, caused the *Washington Herald* to declare the "virtual collapse of the 'third degree' defense" and observe that the government "figures to have clinched the case against Wan."[23]

At that point, having accomplished all they set out to do, the prosecutors rested their case. Then it was O'Shea's turn. First he made several motions to exclude certain exhibits and testimony. All were overruled and exceptions were noted. Then, finally, he offered his opening statement. He contended that Wan's admission of guilt had been extorted and been anything but voluntary. The defendant, he said, had been "cursed, pushed and struck" until he gave the police what they wanted. He had been put through the wringer, despite the fact that he was clearly terribly sick.

"The defendant was in ill health and his condition became so acute that he would have confessed to anything should it result in his being left alone by the detectives," O'Shea asserted. He also promised to show that Wan was not without funds—an answer to the prosecution's assertion that money had been his motive—and that he had had nothing to do with the forgery.[24]

O'Shea's first witness was Tsong Ing Van, who testified that shortly before the murders the brothers had received $500 from their mother and a promise of more and that Wan owned several ruby and jade stickpins valued at $1,600. He did not deny his own role in passing the forged check but told a previously unheard story about where and how he got it that had nothing to do with Wan.

When he left the Harris Hotel in search of fruit for his ailing brother, Van testified, he bumped into two Chinese men who claimed to have met him in Vancouver, though he did not recognize them. One, he said, was called Moy and another was named T. P. Wong. He soon excused himself and returned to his brother's bedside, but the next day when he and Wan were in Union Station about to board a train for New York, he ran into them again. T. P. Wong—whom Van described as looking a lot like his brother, only a bit taller—asked Van to go to Riggs Bank on his behalf to cash a check because he couldn't speak

English well. It had been T. P. Wong, not his brother, who had given him the envelope containing the check and the letter and had waited in the taxicab, Van swore. The rest of his story tracked with the earlier narrative of what had happened at the bank, except that he denied having left Ben Sen Wu's card there.[25]

On cross-examination, U.S. Attorney Laskey asked Van for the address of the two men; he said he didn't know. He also asked why he had told the people at the bank to call the mission to vouch for the check.

"No, I told them to call the house of *T. P. Wong*, not Dr. *T. T. Wong*," he replied.[26]

It was a wholly unsatisfactory account. Why would Van have felt an obligation to help men he did not know? Why would he have left a sick brother in the train station to do the errand? How is it that the strangers just *happened* to have a check from the Chinese Educational Mission and that he just *happened* to run into them twice in two days? And why tell the bank to call a man who couldn't speak English, whose address he didn't know? It all strained credulity.

Van was more believable when he described the interrogations. He recalled the racist epithets the detectives had hurled at his brother. Pullman had pointed a finger in Wan's face and called him a "cold-blooded Chinaman," Van averred. Then he said, "You know what you did. You are very sick; in dying condition. Why don't you say something and let your brother go? Your little brother has a good future; we just want you to say something and let him go out. You tell me you are Christian and love your brother. Why don't you say it and let your brother go?"

By Van's account, Wan never admitted the writing on the check was his. And he recalled it had been the *detectives* who had suggested that Wu had shot the other two men and that they had even added that such a story would be believable because Wu had owned the pistol. They had, in essence, spelled out the story to which they wanted Wan to confess.

Van even turned the clothes hanger story on its head. It was Burlingame who brandished the hanger at Wan and not the other way

FIG. 16. U.S. Attorney for the District of Columbia John E. Laskey, 1905.
Source: Library of Congress, LC-H25-109687-H.

around, he told the jury. He recalled urging Wan, then splayed out on the floor, "Just say yes! They send us back to the hotel and give us food and then don't send us to dungeon." And that was the point at which Wan had relented and the brothers were taken to the police station.

Van was not present for any further interrogation of his brother but he did recall the jubilation of Burlingame and Laws at the jail when they finally secured Wan's signature on the typewritten confession.

Next it was Wan's turn. He spoke in hushed tones when he took the stand on January 6 and had to be asked several times to speak up. He clasped his hands tightly and swayed back and forth in his chair but otherwise betrayed no emotion.

Wan recounted something approaching the narrative he had first related when the detectives brought him to Washington: he had left the mission because he did not want to trouble his hosts but had checked into the Harris Hotel because he was too ill to go home that day. He had summoned his brother to nurse him. He had returned to the mission on the day of the murders because Wu had told him there was a package from China waiting for him there; that was when Kang Li had knocked at the door. But not finding Wu at home, he had left shortly afterward, he said, and returned to the hotel and gone to bed. The brothers had gone back to New York the following day but only after Van had left him at Union Station for a time in order to do an errand. He denied he had ever told the detectives he had left the previous day and insisted that the first time he was aware of the murders was when he read about them in the New York papers.[27]

Wan, of course, painted a far bleaker picture of his interrogation than that to which the detectives had testified earlier, especially the part at the house on Kalorama Road. He repudiated his confession, claiming he was so ill at the time he could not even stand up straight. He denied that his handwriting was on the check stub and allowed only that a few of the letters looked like his writing. He echoed his brother's account of the coat hanger incident and of the threats and profanity used by the detectives. He testified that he was not only asked questions; he was also given suggestions by the detectives. Finally when Grant had submitted that the murder had been a case of self-defense and said, "Just say yes and then we can both rest," he had reached his limit and simply said "yes" so the questions would stop. He had signed the confession knowing it was untrue, he stated, because "if I don't sign it I think they might review the case again and question me again."

When O'Shea asked him point blank whether he had killed Dr. Wong and the others, Wan broke down and sobbed as he denied it.

Laskey was not the only one to cross-examine the witness. The judge joined in as well. He wanted to know why Wan had made incriminating statements when he knew that they would mean the death penalty. Wan explained he had done it to get rid of the police and stop their questions.[28]

"Nobody held a gun over you?" the judge asked.

"Nobody."

"And nobody threatened to kill you?"

"This is worse than killing," Wan replied. "If they kill me, I don't mind."

"You did know what you were signing?"

"Yes."

"And your explanation is that you would rather sign it than go through what you were going through?"

"My idea to sign the confession—they want me to tell and wanted me to confess and to sign, and my idea is this: I want them to leave me alone and let my brother nurse me and let me get well. I don't want to argue with them at the same time."

Dr. James A. Gannon, the physician in charge of the DC jail, took the stand after Wan; it was his testimony that did the most to bolster Wan's case. A Georgetown graduate, he had practiced medicine and surgery for thirteen years. At the prison hospital, he supervised thirty-two physicians of various specialties; it was his responsibility to see all patients with non-trivial illnesses and ensure that they obtained proper treatment.

Dr. Gannon had first met Wan at the jail the day after he arrived. He had found the prisoner weak, exhausted, and emaciated, suffering from intense abdominal pain. He diagnosed the illness as spastic colitis, judged that Wan had been ill for several weeks, and ordered him removed to the Red Cross room, where prisoners too ill to remain in their cells were quartered. The doctor described the ailment—a narrowing of the intestine—and testified that it would result in almost constant pain. He had visited Wan a dozen times after that, he said, and kept him in bed for at least a month.

The judge then more or less took over the cross-examination, which focused on the effect of colitis on Wan's judgment.

"Are you prepared to say that that had any effect on his mind?" the judge asked.

"Oh yes; I am," the doctor replied.

"What do you say; he was of sound or unsound mind?"

"Well, I say in that regard, insofar he was unable to make an important decision, he was of unsound mind."

"Would he know what he was signing?"

"He would know what he was signing, yes."

"Would he be liable to sign a confession that would lead him to the gallows in that condition?"

"I think he would if he wanted to be let alone."

"With spastic colitis, if he was accused of crime he would simply sign a paper and say, 'You hang me'? That is your opinion as a medical man?" the judge asked.

"I say, if he was as sick as that and in as great pain as that, he would do anything to have the torture stopped."

After a few more witnesses were heard, the defense rested and the two sides gave their summations. O'Shea went first. In addition to repeating the arguments against the validity of the confession, he did his best to pick apart the prosecution's case. He observed that if Wan had truly plotted to kill the three men, he would surely have lured Kang Li into the house and killed him as well. And he would have been unlikely to register at the Harris Hotel under his own name or leave a paper trail in the form of telegrams to his brother. A circumstantial case could have been made against Kang Li as easily as it had been made against Wan, he asserted, but the police had exonerated Li too early and thus failed to investigate him thoroughly.

"If they treated this boy as the testimony indicates, it is high time an American jury put its stamp of disapproval on the methods of the police," he said in conclusion.

Laws and Laskey then attacked Wan's credibility by recounting the lies he and his brother had told in the course of their interrogations, pointing out that he had not recanted his confession until he was brought to trial.

"The police would have been derelict in their duty if they had not interrogated Wan at great length," Laskey asserted. "If the police are not to be allowed to question persons suspected of crime, particularly those who have been trapped in conflicting statements and lies, you might as well close up the courthouse," he added.

Late in the morning on Friday, January 9, the judge charged the jury, which retired just after noon and was out for only half an hour. Only two ballots were taken: the first tally was eleven to one favoring conviction. But the twelfth juror was persuaded by his peers in short order and the second ballot was unanimous.[29]

The jury found Wan guilty of murder in the first degree, the penalty for which was death. Wan—who had been so confident of acquittal that he had packed his suitcase in anticipation of leaving Washington immediately—listened to the verdict in stoic silence. He straightened briefly, then crumpled back into his chair and hung his head. He was led out of the courtroom, trembling and sobbing, by his attorney and the bailiff.[30]

8

Appeal

ON HIS RETURN Wan was transferred to one of four double cells in the southeast section of the jailhouse known colloquially as "gallows lane." This was where inmates awaiting execution were housed. His conviction brought their number to five, a new record for the jail. He was assigned the second bed in a cell occupied by forty-six-year-old Charles Ross Webster, who had been convicted of the fatal shooting of a fifteen-year-old boy.[1]

Hard on the heels of the verdict, U.S. Attorney Laskey announced that Wan's brother Van would soon be brought to trial on charges of forgery and "uttering"—that is, knowingly passing—a forged check. Van had been caught in several lies. Wan's jury had not been persuaded by his story that a man he barely knew had given him an envelope with the check inside and that he had known nothing about its contents when he took it to the bank. There was every reason to believe a second jury would feel the same way.[2]

Under the law, Wan had four days to petition Judge Gould for a new trial; O'Shea and his co-counsel, Charles Fahy, announced their intention to file such a motion the following week. Arguments were scheduled for Friday, January 23, but they had to be postponed after Gould slipped on an icy patch of pavement on his way to the mailbox and injured himself, necessitating confinement at home.[3]

Gould's convalescence postponed action on Wan's petition until the court's April term; it was not until May 7 that he ruled on the motion, which, not unexpectedly, relied heavily on the admission of the confession. Wan sat stoically as the judge overruled the petition, asserting that there had been nothing in the testimony to justify the contention that he had been mishandled by the police. The judge even went so far as to compliment the detectives on how they had handled the case, lauding them for employing "unusual detective skill." He also stated his belief that conviction could have been secured even without the confession and scheduled sentencing for the following week.

But there was no mystery in what the sentence would be.[4]

On May 14, 1920, in a crowded courtroom, Wan was told to rise and was asked if he had anything to say prior to sentencing. He stood unsteadily and grasped the table in front of him with both hands for support but declined to speak. At that point, Judge Ashley M. Gould condemned him to death by hanging, to be carried out between 10:00 a.m. and 2:00 p.m. on December 1. At the words, "May the Lord have mercy on your soul," the prisoner collapsed in a dead faint and would have hit the floor had he not been caught by the marshals. It took three of them to carry him from the courtroom to a cell in the courthouse basement, where he was placed on a bench, his head propped up by his wadded overcoat. Revived after a physician administered first aid, he sobbed bitterly, his body shaking with convulsions."

O'Shea gave immediate notice of his intention to appeal.[5]

Wan was taken back to the jail, where he remained ill for three days. The next day came the news that President Woodrow Wilson had commuted the sentence of his cellmate, who was sent to Atlanta Penitentiary for life. Wan may well have wished for the same treatment; apart from favorable action by the District of Columbia Court of Appeals, presidential clemency surely appeared his best hope of being spared the gallows.[6]

The appeals process required that the defense team compile a "bill of exceptions" that set out, in their opinion, the errors made by the judge that would justify a new trial. This document had to be signed by the presiding judge before the case could advance. It took a good deal of time to prepare, however; on several occasions, Wan's attorneys asked for, and were granted, extensions of the deadline. When the date slipped beyond December, reprieves from execution also became necessary. Wan was granted a stay until May 27, 1921.[7]

The days on gallows lane passed slowly for him. His health improved and he gained twenty-five pounds but slept poorly. He did little reading and did not mix much with his fellow inmates, although he did enjoy an occasional game of checkers. His conduct was considered excellent at all times; he did not give his jailers any trouble.[8]

A week before he was to be executed, Judge Gould still had not received the bill of exceptions from his attorneys. And as it turned out, he never would. On May 20, he dropped dead of a heart attack at his Q Street NW home at the age of sixty-one. Wan was just one day from the gallows when another judge was asked to step in. Because the appellate court would not have the opportunity to hear the case until October at the earliest, he deferred the execution until December 9. Nor would that be the last time it would have to be postponed.[9]

In the meantime Wan's cause was taken up by opponents of the death penalty. As part of a campaign to eliminate capital punishment in the District of Columbia, the Anthony League—named for Susan B. Anthony and founded to promote women's suffrage but, having gained it the previous year, now turning its attention to other issues—submitted an appeal to President Warren G. Harding in late May. Calling the death penalty "a barbaric custom of primitive man . . . obnoxious to all Christians since the execution of Christ himself," the petition named the four men then awaiting execution in Washington—Wan among them—and asked the president to commute their sentences. It also called on him to support legislation substituting life imprisonment for all crimes then punishable by death in the District.[10]

Nor was theirs the only voice the president heard. On November 16, a delegation representing various Washington churches and societies called on him at the White House. Headed by Dr. E. O. Watson of the Federal Council of Churches of Christ, and including Episcopalian, Christian Scientist, and Jewish representatives as well as members of the Anthony League, the group presented Harding with a petition declaring that the death penalty was ineffective at deterring crime, hindered convictions, and resulted in the demise of innocents convicted on circumstantial evidence. It requested commutation of the sentences of the four on death row.[11]

Harding could not have been less sympathetic. He didn't even let them finish reading their petition. He interrupted to ask whether he was about to hear an appeal for the commutation of death sentences; when told that he was, he declared that it would be useless to continue. He coldly informed the delegates that he had no time to listen to such pleas and that he did not believe it was his function to interfere with sentences pronounced by a court of law. The chastised visitors, realizing their mission was hopeless, rose and beat a hasty retreat from his office.[12]

At this point Hugh A. O'Donnell decided to see what he might do to aid his former valet. Wan had briefly worked for him several months before the Washington murders. A sometime actor and lecturer, O'Donnell had been employed by newspapers in Chicago, Philadelphia, and Minneapolis and had been brought to New York to serve as assistant business manager of the *New York Times*, a position he held for nearly two decades. A Notre Dame graduate, he was active in Catholic circles and served for a time as president of the Catholic Writers' Guild.

The newspaperman liked the young Chinese man, refused to believe he was guilty, and resolved to do what he could to help him. He asked James A. Nolan, a well-regarded New York attorney, to get involved. Nolan met with Wan in Washington and, once persuaded of his innocence, decided to approach the Harding administration to ask for a fresh review of the case.

Although he did not formally represent Wan, Nolan wrote Harding's attorney general, Harry M. Daugherty, a five-page letter about the case, poking holes in Wan's confession, which he insisted did not square with the facts, and implying that Laskey had been overzealous in his decision to prosecute. He asked that Daugherty investigate the matter:

> I should be very much indebted to you if you would appoint a good lawyer who may be at the same time a good investigator to cooperate with me to determine the truth or falsity further of the facts set down in the paper. The only impartial course if I could be permitted to suggest in my humble opinion, would be to appoint someone wholly detached from the previous history of the case and go at the matter from beginning to end, as I have been trying to do.

Nolan also copied the secretary of state and the president on his letter; the White House staff merely referred it to the Justice Department, which didn't quite know what to make of the request. After all, a jury had already found Wan guilty of murder. In a reply penned by an assistant attorney general, the department interpreted the entreaty as an application for executive clemency, noting that, as the case had not been finally adjudicated by the courts, any appeal for a pardon would be premature.[13]

When Major Peyton Gordon succeeded John E. Laskey as U.S. attorney for the District of Columbia in August, nearly 1,500 cases awaited his attention on day one. A World War I veteran and a former pardon attorney, Gordon had been in private practice before his appointment. He worked steadily through his backlog and eventually got to the *Wan* case.

The government had taken issue with the bill of exceptions as drawn up by the defense, insisting on revisions to the document. That, together with the death of the trial judge, had severely retarded progress on the case.[14] When Walter I. McCoy, chief justice of the DC Supreme Court, finally signed off on it, however, he did so over the objection of O'Shea, who wished to use the fact that McCoy had not been the presiding judge at the original trial as a pretext for demanding a new one. By the end of 1921, Wan's appeal still had not proceeded to the appellate court. On December 7, with only two days to spare, he was granted a third stay of execution, until April 7, 1922.[15]

The appellant's brief—prepared by O'Shea, Fahy, and John I. Sacks, Wan's attorneys—ran for 140 pages and chronicled 127 ostensible errors by the trial court. That of the appellee, prepared by Gordon and Assistant U.S. Attorney Joseph H. Bilbrey—Bolitha J. Laws had stepped down in 1920—was only fifty-six pages long, but it succinctly set out the government's positions on the points in contention.

It took another year—and three more stays of execution—before the Court of Appeals of the District of Columbia finally heard the case of *Ziang Sung Wan v. United States*. A few days before it rendered its decision, the check-uttering case against Wan's brother Van came before the DC Supreme Court but was deferred. The U.S. attorney's office

FIG. 17. U.S. Attorney for the District of Columbia Peyton Gordon, 1923.
Source: Library of Congress, LC-F8-23747.

decided to postpone prosecution of Van, pending the result of Wan's appeal. The two cases were so closely related and relied on so much of the same evidence that it was easy to see that as one case went so, likely, would go the other. Van remained at liberty on $3,000 bond.[16]

On May 7, 1923—more than three years after Wan's guilty verdict—the Court of Appeals handed down its decision. Judge Josiah Alexander Van Orsdel, a former assistant attorney general and strict constructionist who had received a recess appointment from President Theodore Roosevelt in 1907 and had sat on the court since that time, wrote the opinion.

Judge Van Orsdel disposed in short order of the smaller issues raised in the appeal. It was clear that the fundamental question before the court was whether Wan's confession should have been admitted into evidence at all. In their brief, his attorneys argued that

> the statements were not the free and voluntary statements of the accused, only such statements being admissible, but the unwilling, painful and at last desperate product of the mind of a Chinese youth whose body was racked by a painful illness, further weakened by ten days of questioning, suspicion and accusation, include one all night questioning in the house of murder itself, and whose mind was unwillingly and involuntarily led under the domination of four detectives finally and hopelessly to surrender to their will after a long drawn out period of skillful mental coercion, charged one minute with hope, then with fear, now with kindness, then with trickery and feigned kindness, always with recklessness, the like of which we believe has not come to light in the printed records of a Court in modern times.[17]

To bolster their assertion that only "free and voluntary statements" were admissible, Wan's lawyers cited the 1897 Supreme Court case of *Bram v. United States*, which concerned a murder on an American vessel on the high seas. When the ship had reached Halifax, Nova Scotia, the defendant had been stripped and searched and taken into custody. Understanding himself to be a prisoner bound to obey all orders he was given, he gave a statement to a police detective that was later used against him in court.

The court had thrown out Bram's confession, ruling that

> a confession, in order to be admissible, must be free and voluntary; that is, must not be extracted by any sort of threats or violence, nor obtained by any direct or implied promises however slight, nor by the exertion of any improper influence . . . for the law cannot measure the force of the influence used, or decide upon its effect upon the mind of the prisoner, and therefore excludes the declaration if any degree of influence has been exerted.[18]

The *Bram* case wasn't actually the first time the court had ruled on this issue. More than a dozen years earlier, in *Hopt v. People of the Territory of Utah*, it had cited an eighteenth-century test from an English common law precedent that admitted all confessions as voluntary *except* in cases where there was evidence they had been elicited by threats or inducements sufficient to overcome a defendant's free will.[19] This common law standard had proceeded from the assumption that coerced confessions were not reliable or trustworthy.[20]

In its *Bram* ruling, the court had expanded the rule articulated in *Hopt*, making it clear that a variety of police behaviors could render a confession involuntary; one needed to look at *all* the circumstances surrounding an interrogation to determine whether the will of the accused had been compromised. But more importantly, the court established a firmer legal underpinning for the voluntariness test than mere common law precedents that could easily be overridden by legislation, as in fact had happened in at least one state.

The court did not negate the common law test but found additional, and more potent, authority for it in the Constitution itself:

> In criminal trials, in the courts of the United States, wherever a question arises whether a confession is incompetent because not voluntary, the issue is controlled by that portion of the Fifth Amendment to the Constitution of the United States commanding that no person "shall be compelled in any criminal case to be a witness against himself."[21]

In other words, the Constitution supported the contention that confessions induced by promises or threats were by definition involuntary and hence inadmissible. But the justification for excluding them was not that they were *unreliable*, but that defendants enjoyed a *right* under the Fifth Amendment that required they be thrown out.[22]

It had taken some legal gymnastics to get here, because the Fifth Amendment does not directly address the question of police coercion or the voluntariness of confessions. But the court reasoned that coerced confessions were against the spirit of the amendment, which had "crystallized" many rights for accused persons, even some not specifically enumerated. In the court's own language:

A brief consideration of the reasons which gave rise to the adoption of the Fifth Amendment, of the wrongs which it was intended to prevent, and the safeguards which it was its purpose unalterably to secure, will make it clear that the generic language of the amendment was but a crystallization when the amendment was adopted.[23]

Since the District of Columbia fell under federal jurisdiction, there was no question that the Constitution applied to Wan's case. So the principal question the appellate court considered in the *Wan* case was whether the Chinese man had been so induced when he made his statement to the detectives.[24]

Surprisingly, the District of Columbia Court of Appeals found that he had not. Judge Van Orsdel wrote that the admissibility of the confession was "supported by every principle of law," or at least that "the evidence tending to show that it was involuntarily made was not so conclusive as to justify the court in excluding the confession from the jury." He added:

> While he undoubtedly thought that leniency and mercy might result from confession, his excuse for making it is that they importuned him with questions and used abusive language toward him, neither of which are in the category of promise or threat.[25]

And so the guilty verdict was sustained. Accordingly a week after the appellate court's decision, the trial court issued a warrant for the execution of Ziang Sung Wan and set a date for his hanging three days later. But on motion of counsel O'Shea, Wan received a sixty-day stay. At the same time, he announced that Wan intended to appeal the decision to the U.S. Supreme Court.[26]

It would be a long shot but there weren't any other options.

9

The Third Degree

THE U.S. SUPREME Court had addressed the admissibility of confessions in a federal court in 1897 in the *Bram* case. It had ruled that the appropriate test was whether any promises or threats had been made by law enforcement officers or any other actions had induced the confession to the point that it could not be considered voluntary. The court had also ruled that authority for this test could be found not only in common law but in the Fifth Amendment.

So why would the court accept another case that covered essentially the same ground?

In the quarter-century that had passed since *Bram*, the country had been embroiled in a robust national debate about the ethics and efficacy of what had come to be called the "third degree." It was no accident that attorney O'Shea had made certain to ask all potential jurors in Wan's 1919 trial if they would be willing to send a defendant to his death based solely on a confession obtained after extensive grilling. He was certain many would say no.

Although the practice of extracting confessions through intensive interrogation—if not the rack and the thumbscrew—dates from antiquity, what happened to Wan and his brother at the Fifteenth Street clinic, the Dewey Hotel, and the mission house acquired its modern name shortly before the turn of the twentieth century. In 1895, the *New York World*, in an article about a man accused of murdering his wife, noted that he had been taken to police headquarters and subjected to "the famous 'Third Degree.'"[1]

The term's definition, however, was imprecise. In 1901, the *New York Times* explained it as "the big examination given . . . at Headquarters by the chief of the Detective Bureau," following questioning by an officer at the police station house or a detective in police court. A decade later, District of Columbia chief of police, Richard H. Sylvester, suggested that it referred to intensive interrogation of a suspect "in private quarters," as opposed to first- and second-degree questioning done upon arrest and at the "place of confinement," respectively.

Some cited Freemasonry as the source of the expression, as the process of becoming a "third-degree master mason" involved interrogation.[2] The *Times*, however, argued that it had everything to do with degrees of heat. The paper recounted the interrogation at Manhattan's Leonard Street Police Station of a man named Brunt, who had been arrested for the theft of bonds from his employer. The story, which supposedly dated from the 1860s, may have been apocryphal, as contemporary newspapers do not seem to have covered it. But as the *Times* recalled it, the police were convinced of Brunt's guilt. To elicit a confession, the captain ordered a stove placed in his cell and instructed the guards to keep the coals stoked despite the fact that it was August. Even after the temperature in the enclosure surpassed 100 degrees Fahrenheit, Brunt refused to crack. But after suffering for three weeks and losing twenty-three pounds, he was at death's door and finally relented.[3]

Closely related to that technique was the "sweatbox," a six-foot-square cell in which blankets were used to block all light. Over a period of several days, this practice induced "a depression that amounted to suffocation." It gave rise to the expression "to sweat a confession" out of someone.

Creative detectives came up with many other methods, some of which amounted to nothing short of torture. These included salting bread given to prisoners and subsequently withholding water and rigging an electronic device to tap a sheet of glass rhythmically and relentlessly for hours on end. One suspect picked up by the Chicago police was confined to a damp, pitch-dark basement cell. When after four days he refused to give information, his keepers released a box of red ants, which bit him repeatedly, and blew red pepper into his cell, causing him extreme distress. He also reported being doused with scalding water.[4]

As these techniques and others like them were exposed in the newspapers, they evoked strong reactions, some positive but most negative. To some, such extraordinary methods were justifiable if the crime was particularly heinous. Buffalo police did not deny they had tortured Leon Czolgosz, the anarchist who had initially refused to say a word after his arrest for the fatal shooting of President William McKinley in 1901. It is not entirely clear what was done to him, but Superintendent of Police William S. Bull received no shortage of letters offering creative—and alarmingly bloodthirsty—suggestions for what *might* be done.[5]

The strongest supporters of the third degree were the police; in the service of defending it, many took pains to make it sound as benign as possible. In 1905 Thomas Byrnes, former chief of detectives of the New York Police Department, described a genial process worlds removed from the sweatbox. The ingredients of his "mental fencing match" included arousing the sympathy of the accused (because "the most hardened criminal always has some remnants of a conscience left"), avoiding censure or accusation and treating the offense lightly ("something that might happen to anybody"), and drawing the suspect out ("chattering away about all manner of subjects" until "the fellow became as putty in the hands of an adroit examiner").

Byrnes called this technique "a vital necessity to the Police Department in the detection of crimes" because even when it failed to elicit the desired information it always revealed some new aspect of the crime.[6] But other officers of the law denied that it existed at all. Theodore A. Bingham, New York City police commissioner from 1906 to 1909, blamed the newspapers for exaggerating the practice, at least as far as New York was concerned; his successor, William F. Baker, agreed, maintaining that "the sweating or third degree system is an imaginary something derived from the brain of some bright news writer."[7]

Overall, however, the popular view of the third degree was overwhelmingly critical. As early as 1902 the *Times* called for its abolition:

Such proceedings . . . cannot be too strongly denounced. They violate every principle of law, reason, humanity, and personal right. They restore the barbarity of ancient and mediaeval methods. They obstruct, instead of advance, the proper ascertainment of truth.[8]

Many editorials sounding similar themes followed in subsequent years. "Is it possible that any treatment of persons accused of crime in this humane age can be in any way comparable with the atrocities practiced four or five centuries ago, when human rights had but little recognition and human suffering excited but scant sympathy?" the *Baltimore Sun* asked rhetorically. The *Spokane Press* lamented the fact that the United States was the only civilized nation where the practice survived. And the *Pittsburgh Press* opined, "It is un-American; it is more—it is brutal. It is criminal, too, and American juries are coming more and more to realize that fact."[9]

Even a Broadway play did its part to stoke the coals. Entitled *The Third Degree* and written by Charles Klein, a well-known playwright and actor, it portrayed the use of hypnotism and seven hours of interrogation to wring a confession from an innocent murder suspect. The compelling drama, which opened in February 1909 and was performed in many cities around the country, was so powerful that the *Tacoma Times* predicted that members of the audience, after seeing it, would vote overwhelmingly to acquit a local woman who had recently recanted a confession that she had killed her husband. The play was made into a motion picture more than once during the silent era, most notably in 1919 and 1926.[10]

A few months after the debut of Klein's play, the practice was very much in the national news because of a murder case that ironically also involved a Chinese. After the half-clothed, partially decomposed body of Elsie Sigel, a twenty-two-year-old white missionary working in New York's Chinatown, was discovered inside a steamer trunk above a chop suey restaurant, a national manhunt was launched for the killer. The principal suspect, a Chinese man with whom the young woman had been having a love affair, had disappeared together with a friend. Although he was never apprehended, police did nab his companion, a man named Chong Sing.

Chong was subjected to a thirty-hour, marathon examination during which he was "interrogated, bullied, persuaded and entangled in a mass of questions," according to the *San Francisco Call*. "It was not until late, however, that his spirit was sufficiently broken or sufficient inducements were offered for him to cast aside his air of

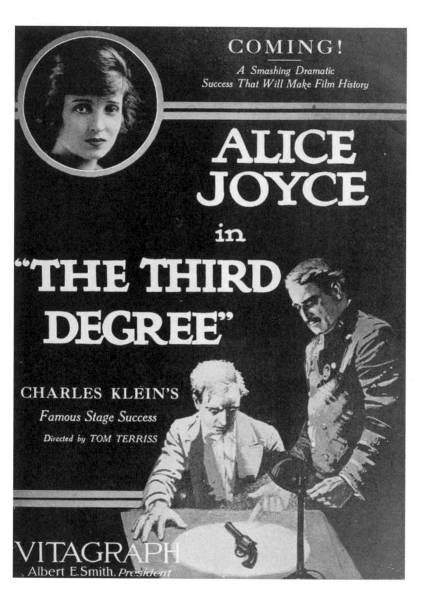

FIG. 18. An advertisement for Charles Klein's play, *The Third Degree*.
Source: *Moving Picture World*.

stolidness and tell of the death of the young missionary."[11] It didn't
help that Chong was Chinese; like blacks and other minorities, Chinese were looked down upon and generally suffered far more than
whites in such situations.

In a brutal editorial that could just as well have been written a decade later about the *Wan* case, the *New York Times* opined that

> about the only thing that could possibly excite even a trace of public sympathy for a Chinese plausibly suspected of taking part in or aiding to conceal such a murder as that of Elsie Sigel would be the underlying conviction that such treatment as that to which the man Chung [*sic*] has been subjected by the police is both morally and legally wrong . . . For torture it is to keep a man awake for thirty consecutive hours, plied all that time by relays of questioners who use all sorts of threats and deceptions to make him admit the correctness of a preconceived assumption as to his guilt or guilty knowledge.[12]

It is worth noting that Chong later recanted his confession.

Denunciation of the third degree had reached such a fever pitch by 1910 that the U.S. Senate launched a wide-ranging investigation into its use by the federal government. It chartered a select committee in April that year and charged it with inquiring into "the alleged practice of administering what is known as the 'third degree' ordeal by officers or employees of the United States for the purpose of extorting from those charged with crime statements and confessions."[13]

Republican senator Frank B. Brandegee of Connecticut, chair of the committee, let it be known that the body was open to hearing any complaints that fell under its aegis, from all comers. But because criminal justice was still largely a state-level concern, the Brandegee Committee, as it was known, was limited in its jurisdiction to federal law enforcement officials, including Secret Service agents, federal marshals, and U.S. attorneys. It heard many complaints against the Washington DC Police Department, which was also under the federal government, but most had more to do with police brutality than abuse of the third degree per se.[14]

The head of the Secret Service denied that the practice was used among federal law enforcement officials; even George W. Wickersham, attorney general of the United States, testified that he had "never heard of the use of the so-called 'third degree,' by any Federal official." Many years later, after studying the matter, Wickersham would come to a strikingly different conclusion.[15]

A recommendation to strengthen extradition laws was included in the committee's final report to the Senate on August 4, 1911, which ran for a paltry four pages, but not much else was urged, probably because of the limited jurisdiction of the body. Had the members been in a position to consider (and legislate about) the activities of state and local police and courts, they surely would have found much worthy of regulation. But criminal law enforcement was essentially still left to the states in 1910.[16]

Apart from the public discourse on the third degree, there was also a fierce debate in the judiciary as to what kinds of interrogations and police conduct were actually prohibited by *Bram*. In retaining the common law test concerning promises and threats but broadening the definition of voluntariness and finding constitutional authority for it, the *Bram* court had in essence offered subsequent judges a smorgasbord of options. Federal judges were bound by the decision, but that did not stop them from continuing to wrestle with what it meant; a creative judge might find justification in it for however he chose to rule. Jurists in District of Columbia courts were particularly recalcitrant, frequently admitting suspect confessions. That was precisely what happened in the *Wan* case: the determination of whether his confession was coerced had been left up to the jury.

The state courts, for their part, were not constrained by the *Bram* decision. The framers had not intended that the Constitution govern the internal affairs of the states; the process of applying the Bill of Rights to state and local government procedures was a tricky one that played out, right by right and clause by clause, from the period following the Civil War well into the 1960s. As a practical matter, however, many accepted *Bram*'s underlying reasoning and were guided by it. In the period leading up to the *Wan* case, in fact, state courts cited *Bram* as a precedent no fewer than fifty-eight times. But there was little consistency in how, or even if, they applied it. In 1909, the Supreme Court of the State of Washington ordered a new trial for a defendant convicted of hiring his brother to kill his fiancée. He had been "sweated" to induce a confession.[17] By contrast, the following year a district court judge in Utah admitted a confession by a man accused of murdering a Salt Lake City police officer, despite the fact that it was offered, the defendant maintained, after he had been stripped naked, thrown into a damp, cement-floored cell, and denied food and water for two days.[18]

The year 1922 saw the publication of a national survey on practices employed by local authorities to obtain confessions. It was compiled by two prison reform experts: B. Ogden Chisolm, who would soon be appointed by President Coolidge to represent the United States at the International Prison Commission, and Hastings H. Hart, president of the American Prison Association. The study sought to determine whether local prosecutors and police normally advised suspects of their rights, how far they went in promising leniency or immunity in exchange for information, their view of the proper limits to "grilling," and whether they believed using threats or causing physical suffering was "advisable." Sixty-six replies were received from twenty-eight district or prosecuting attorneys and thirty-eight chiefs of police representing fifty-one cities in twenty-seven states.

In only five of the states was there legislation on the books to regulate the preliminary investigation of suspects; in only seven cities were there local police rules to govern this. In thirty-four cities the practice was left entirely to the discretion of law enforcement officers. Only five of twenty-eight prosecutors favored legislation to regulate such interrogations; most feared new restrictions would hinder prosecutions. Seven maintained that the proscription against compelling suspects to testify against themselves did not apply to initial investigations outside of a courtroom. All disapproved of physical coercion and torture, but more than half sanctioned "severe grilling," whatever that was.[19]

If the U.S. Supreme Court chose to hear Wan's appeal, it could find ample justification not only in the facts of the case and in public sentiment but in the crying need to bring order to the chaos surrounding confessions then reigning in the judicial system. Such a hodgepodge of laws and policies in a nation where individual states enjoyed autonomy in setting rules for criminal procedure was inevitable but it was also problematic. There was a clear disconnect between the views of most law enforcement officers about the third degree, on the one hand, and public opinion, on the other. The courts had been given guidance on how to deal with coerced confessions but permitted plenty of room for interpretation and misinterpretation.

Exactly what constituted "voluntariness" was anything but clear.

10

The Supreme Court

THE DISTRICT OF Columbia Court of Appeals, which had plowed in so completely behind the trial court judge, was not supportive of a petition to the U.S. Supreme Court. On May 27, Judge Van Orsdel denied O'Shea a writ of error, which essentially meant he was satisfied that all outstanding issues had been resolved, and declined to join the defense in requesting further review of the case. This was not an insurmountable obstacle, however: O'Shea could still appeal directly to the Supreme Court without Van Orsdel's concurrence; he and his colleagues immediately began preparations to do just that.[1]

Although O'Shea was admitted to the Supreme Court bar and had argued cases before the body in the past, with so much at stake it must surely have seemed prudent to augment the defense team with heavier hitters. But there was the stubborn fact that the Chinese brothers were essentially penniless. It is unclear how they had even managed to pay their attorneys up to this point, since Wan said later that they had not informed their mother, who could have bankrolled their defense, of their predicament. It is probably a safe bet that the lawyers had worked for little or no compensation, or else had been appointed by the court and were being paid by the government. If a patron had stepped in to compensate them for their efforts, there is no record of it.

But two champions *did* step in at this point, when the Supreme Court appeared to be Wan's last hope, and neither was a rich man or an attorney. One was Wan's former employer, *New York Times* executive Hugh A. O'Donnell, who had already asked an attorney friend to intervene on Wan's behalf. The other was a Catholic priest by the name of the Reverend Peter J. O'Callaghan. A Harvard graduate and a temperance advocate, Father O'Callaghan headed the Apostolic Mission House, a training school for missionaries located at Catholic University in northeast Washington DC. He had gotten to know Wan at the suggestion of a Maryknoll priest who was a friend of O'Donnell's. A decade earlier, O'Callaghan had garnered national publicity by helping secure a pardon for Herman Billik, a Bohemian fortune-teller condemned to death for a half-dozen murders in Illinois whose conviction the Supreme Court had declined to overturn.

The immutable opposition of the Catholic Church to the death penalty likely played a part in O'Callaghan's decision to take up Wan's cause but there is no doubt he believed in the Chinese man's innocence. He had visited Wan at the District jail many times and said later that he "felt instinctively that he could not be guilty," adding that "I had known and talked to many murderers, and I knew the murderer type. Wan was not that type." Nor did the priest care that Wan was not a Roman Catholic.[2]

O'Donnell and O'Callaghan raised a small sum to pay for court fees but their major contribution was to draft several eminent attorneys to help bring Wan's case to the Supreme Court on a pro bono basis.[3] Thanks to their efforts, O'Shea and Fahy, who continued to anchor Wan's team together with Frederic D. McKenney (one of the named partners in O'Shea's law firm), were joined by William Cullen Dennis, a former State Department lawyer and sometime legal adviser to the Chinese government.

O'Callaghan's biggest coup, however, was recruiting John W. Davis, former congressman, solicitor general of the United States, and ambassador to Great Britain. Davis had argued seventy-three cases before the Supreme Court during his term at the Justice Department and many others while in private practice. Davis was a Washington luminary. The following year he would become the Democratic Party's nominee for president and mount an unsuccessful challenge to unseat incumbent Calvin Coolidge.

The normal procedure for requesting judicial review by the Supreme Court was to petition for a writ of certiorari, an order to a lower court to submit the record of a case for higher-level scrutiny. The Supreme Court is under no obligation to act on such petitions and does so

FIG. 19. John W. Davis, 1924. Source: Library of Congress, LC-H25-132648-D.

purely at its discretion but, despite the fact that the court had already considered the issue of voluntary confessions in the *Bram* case and had paid precious little attention to it since that time, O'Shea was oddly confident the justices would accept Wan's case. The appeal was filed on July 23, 1923; on the same day Wan's execution was postponed yet again, this time to November 23.

In the petition, the attorneys recapped the salient points of the case.

But the basis for this appeal was far narrower than that of the earlier one. As was customary with Supreme Court petitions, it focused on one key issue, in this case the admissibility of Wan's confession; it did not repeat all the other objections raised and rejected in the initial appeal. The basic argument was that the appellate court, while citing the *Bram* case in its decision, had not drawn the proper lessons from it:

> Although the opinion of this Court in the Bram case was repeatedly referred to and at great length quoted from in the course of argument on appeal before the learned Court of Appeals of the District of Columbia, that learned tribunal seemingly thought it unnecessary to advert to petitioner's arguments based thereon . . . contenting itself with pointing out the views of other courts, as well as its own, as to the differences in definitions of "confessions," "admissions," from which guilt might be logically inferred and "casual observations" which "an innocent bystander might logically have made," and referred to Bram . . . only in passing.[4]

No doubt the attorneys hoped to interest the court in the case by focusing its attention on a point of law the justices might agree was one of national significance that needed clarification. They also made it very clear that the case was a matter of life and death.

Former president William Howard Taft had realized a lifelong ambition when he was named chief justice of the Supreme Court by President Harding in 1921; he was confirmed by the Senate on the very day of his nomination and served for the balance of the decade. It was said that he much preferred that role to his earlier job as president. The other justices on the court in 1924 were Willis Van Devanter, Pierce Butler, Joseph McKenna, George Sutherland, Oliver Wendell Holmes Jr., Edward Terry Sanford, James Clark McReynolds, and Louis D. Brandeis. They were, in the main, economically conservative men who favored limiting the power of the federal government and who were activist in protecting business over labor interests.

By contrast, the Taft court was fairly passive on civil liberties, if not hostile to them. The protections for accused persons enshrined in the Bill of Rights had not yet been applied to the states; as a body these justices did not see it as their role to effect such change. With occasional exceptions, they were content to leave criminal matters to the states. Most of their deliberations in the area of criminal procedure were therefore confined to federal cases like the *Wan* case. They often ruled against defendants.

In *United States v. Lanza*, for example, the Taft court had decided that the Fifth Amendment's proscription against double jeopardy did not prohibit consecutive trials for the same offense in state and federal courts. In *Olmstead v. United States*, the majority would find that warrantless wiretaps obtained by federal agents could be used as evidence in court and did not violate defendants' rights under the Fourth or Fifth amendments. The Court would similarly permit warrantless searches of automobiles in *Carroll v. United States*. And in *Hester v. United States*, it would find that, although the Fourth Amendment prohibited unreasonable searches of "persons, houses, papers, and effects," it did not apply to open fields.[5]

A betting man would not have liked the odds of obtaining a favorable verdict for Ziang Sung Wan from the Taft court. But from the court's point of view, apart from growing public outrage over the use of the third degree, there were some excellent legal reasons to accept the case.

First of all, the failure of the Court of Appeals to rule Wan's confession inadmissible, in spite of staggering evidence that it had been coerced, appeared an egregious departure from voluntariness by almost any definition. There was plenty of reason to believe it had misinterpreted *Bram*. The Supreme Court, it would become clear later, was appalled at the conduct of the Washington police, who had manifestly trampled on Wan's rights. In addition, of course, a man's life hung in the balance.

Second, a generation had passed since the court had opined on coerced confessions and it was clear that the issue was in no way settled. The *Bram* case had implicitly left lower courts to consider the "totality of circumstances" in assessing the voluntariness of confessions but this was such a vague standard that determinations had more or less to be made on a case-by-case basis. The jumble *Bram* left in its wake had allowed the voluntariness standard to be pushed,

Fɪɢ. 20. The Supreme Court in 1924. *Back row, left to right:*
Justices Pierce Butler, Louis D. Brandeis, George Sutherland, and Edward
Terry Sanford. *Front row, left to right:* Justices Willis Van Devanter and
Joseph McKenna, Chief Justice William Howard Taft, and Justices
Oliver Wendell Holmes Jr. and James Clark McReynolds.
Source: Library of Congress, ʟᴄ-ᴜsᴢ62-91090.

pulled, and pummeled in all directions. More definition and clarity were needed.

The *Wan* case may also have been appealing as a vehicle for the court to address the voluntariness principle precisely because Wan was not tortured in any *physical* sense, apart from being questioned incessantly while his colitis flared up. No beatings had taken place, nor had he been "sweated" to induce a confession. The case therefore provided a made-to-order opportunity for the court to make clear that coercion was a far more subtle concept than the rack and the thumbscrew, and could exist even apart from police promises or threats.

The government did not file a brief opposing Wan's attorneys' request for a writ of certiorari; on October 15, 1923, the Supreme Court agreed to hear the case. Wan's execution was again stayed, this time until March 1924. The Justice Department took note of the fact that no less a light than John W. Davis was named on the petition and, perhaps because of his stature, requested the following month that the court hear it at the earliest practicable date. The clerk of the court obligingly put it on the calendar for January 7, 1924.[6] But in December McKenney was forced to request a postponement because William Cullen Dennis, who was to join him in oral arguments, could not finish his government business in London in time to get home to prepare. The court then rescheduled the case for March 3.[7]

But even the March date was pushing things. Wan's team was three weeks late in getting the petitioner's brief to U.S. Attorney Gordon. Dennis did not deliver even an incomplete draft until February 27; he showed up with the rest only on the afternoon of March 1, which permitted only two days for preparation of the government's brief. The Justice Department was forced to ask for another deferral.[8] Accordingly, oral arguments were moved to April 7–8 and Wan was granted yet another stay, until late June.[9]

On those two days in April attorneys McKenney and Dennis presented oral arguments on behalf of Wan, while U.S. Attorney Peyton Gordon represented the United States. The venue was the Old Senate Chamber in the Capitol Building, the hall in which the Supreme Court had convened since 1860, when the Senate had vacated it in favor of its current chamber. The court would not relocate to its neoclassical home across First Street NE—another outstanding manifestation of the City Beautiful movement—until 1935.

Neither the arguments nor the justices' questions were recorded but after they were finished the defense team liked their chances. Dennis wrote Fahy in May of the "hopeful view which we have had of the case since the argument." Then the waiting game began. Anticipating news, Dennis went to the court nearly every decision day following the oral arguments. He was optimistic there would be action in May but was doomed to disappointment. The court adjourned for the summer on June 9 without any ruling in the case or any explanation. Wan, who was corresponding constantly with Fahy, was on tenterhooks of course, so Dennis went to see him in jail to warn him against making any unfavorable inferences from the delay.[10]

As Dennis wrote Fahy after the adjournment:

It seems to me that the delay probably means that the court is going into the matter with the utmost care and preparing to write a fundamental opinion dealing with the whole question of confessions and the modern development of the "third degree." This means what we have always believed, that Wan's case is going to have the careful attention of the court, and I cannot but believe that this will mean a reversal. At any rate, it means that we have done all that lawyers can do, namely, we have secured the very serious consideration of our case by the Supreme Court of the United States.[11]

While waiting for the ruling, Dennis, who counted the Chinese government among his clients, had occasion to meet with Ziang-Ling Chang, the Chinese consul general in New York, as well as several other Chinese officials. He took the opportunity to brief them on the case. China's diplomats in America had not been sympathetic to Wan, who, after all, had been convicted of murdering one of their colleagues and was suspected of killing two others. The *New York Times* even reported a rumor that the Chinese government had spent a considerable sum to aid in prosecuting him and that his widowed mother's property had been confiscated in Shanghai, although there is no evidence for either claim. Dennis felt he had made some headway in gaining sympathy for Wan with his countrymen in the United States, and even brought Chang to call on Wan in jail in mid-May.[12]

As the summer dragged on, Wan tried to be patient. He even wrote Fahy that he was pleased that the court was devoting more time to his case. He corresponded with several friends, noting his pleasure at the news that John W. Davis had been nominated for president (a dark horse candidate, Davis had been chosen to head his party's ticket at the Democratic Convention on the one hundred and third ballot) and his dismay at reports of civil war in China with skirmishes just twelve miles from his home in Shanghai. He had a visit from his brother and was again granted a reprieve from the gallows, this time until October 24.[13]

The Supreme Court had actually decided the case of *Ziang Sung Wan v. United States* at a justices' conference held just four days after the oral arguments, when six of the nine justices voted to reverse the decision of the appellate court. This was, of course, not announced at the time, as they remained free to change their votes after reviewing the draft opinion. Justice Pierce Butler recorded in his docket book that only Justices Sutherland, Van Devanter, and McKenna were opposed. Chief Justice Taft then assigned the task of drafting the opinion to Justice Louis D. Brandeis.[14]

Brandeis was the ideal choice to write the ruling. The Harvard-educated jurist was an unapologetic progressive and civil libertarian. Unlike several of his colleagues on the court, he was a tireless fighter for social justice, freedom of speech, and the right to privacy. While in private practice, he sometimes worked pro bono if a case involved a cause in which he believed. Nominated by President Woodrow Wilson in 1916, he had been the first Jew ever proposed for the court.

April arguments did not leave sufficient time for Brandeis, a wordsmith and a perfectionist, to finish the opinion before the court adjourned for the summer. In fact, he had barely begun work on it by then. As was his practice, the justice wrote out his notes and his initial drafts in longhand on legal pads with a fountain pen. His penmanship, at once bold and difficult to decipher, posed a constant challenge to the court printer, who received a written draft by messenger at the end of each work day and was expected to set it in type by the following morning. Brandeis would then edit the printed version and return it, together with any new material written out in longhand, at the end of the day for another go-around.[15]

Brandeis's extensive notes testify to a laborious and time-consuming process that involved copious research, multiple drafts, and countless edits. His files show that he began work on the opinion on June 2 and went through ten versions before he was satisfied. He labored throughout the month but took a break after July 4, resuming work in mid-September. Finally, on September 24, he ordered copies distributed to his fellow justices. According to the court's tradition, each was to review the document and send a "return" back to the scribe indicating whether he concurred and offering any comments or amendments.

The final document was exceptionally well written; those who had voted with the majority in April all wrote back in support. Justice Holmes, who was in such enthusiastic agreement that he scrib-

FIG. 21. Justice Louis D. Brandeis. Source: Library of Congress,
LC-H25-16601-CD.

bled "Yessirree" on his return, commended Brandeis for his restraint:
"I suppose you are right not to show disgust or wrath—I don't know
whether I could have held [it] in." But Chief Justice Taft, also a supporter from the start, nonetheless betrayed some disquiet over whether
the decision might be setting a troublesome precedent.

"I think this case as you conclusively show is so exceptional," he noted, "that it can not return to plague us in other cases."[16] In retrospect, this seems a naïve comment, for this was no narrow decision. Brandeis was mandating a far broader definition than had been employed in the past, which was bound to affect multitudes of future cases. In the decades since the ruling, it has been cited in twenty-two Supreme Court decisions.

In the end, even the three dissenting justices decided to join the majority and make the decision unanimous. Justice Sutherland complimented Brandeis in his return and added, "I voted the other way but probably shall acquiesce." And even Justice McReynolds, who was such a virulent anti-Semite that he had not so much as uttered a word to Brandeis during the latter's first three years on the court, changed his mind, writing simply, "I shall not oppose."

Wan was not in the courtroom when the Supreme Court finally spoke on October 13, but his brother Van was. The relatively brief decision, issued almost a year to the day after the court agreed to hear the case, was a wide-ranging ruling that was everything his attorneys could have asked for. In carefully chosen language, Brandeis set the stage by recounting evocatively the situation surrounding Wan's confession:

> Wan was held in the hotel room without formal arrest, incommunicado. But he was not left alone. Every moment of the day, and of the night, at least one member of the police force was on guard inside his room. Three ordinary policemen were assigned to this duty. Each served eight hours; the shifts beginning at midnight, at 8 in the morning, and at 4 in the afternoon. Morning, afternoon, and evening (and at least on one occasion after midnight) the prisoner was visited by the superintendent of police and/or one or more of the detectives. The sole purpose of these visits was to interrogate him. Regardless of Wan's wishes and protest, his condition of health, or the hour, they engaged him in conversation. He was subjected to persistent, lengthy, and repeated cross-examination. Sometimes it was subtle, sometimes severe. Always the examination was conducted with a view to entrapping Wan into a confession of his own guilt and/or that of his brother. Whenever these visitors entered the room, the guard was stationed outside the closed door.

On the eighth day, the accusatory questioning took a more excruciating form. A detective was in attendance throughout the day. In the evening, Wan was taken from Hotel Dewey to the Mission. There, continuously for ten hours, this sick man was led from floor to floor minutely to examine and re-examine the scene of the triple murder and every object connected with it, to give explanations, and to answer questions . . . Concerning every object, every incident detailed, he was, in the presence of a stenographer, plied with questions by the superintendent of police and the detectives. By these he was engaged in argument; sometimes separately, sometimes in joint attack. The process of interrogation became ever more insistent. It passed at times from inquiry into command. From 7 o'clock in the evening until 5 o'clock in the morning the questioning continued. Before it was concluded, Li, who was again in attendance, had left the Mission about midnight, worn out by the long hours. The superintendent of police had returned to his home, apparently exhausted. One of the detectives had fallen asleep. To Wan, not a moment of sleep was allowed.

Brandeis then described Wan's physical condition at the end of the interrogation, when he was diagnosed with spastic colitis. He painted a pathetic picture of a weak, exhausted man, unable to eat for days, experiencing constant abdominal pain, constipation, and frequent vomiting. He noted that on the day Wan confessed, he had been interrogated continuously for ten hours and not been allowed a moment of sleep. He quoted the doctor who had examined Wan as testifying that in such a condition he would have been liable to sign even a confession that would lead him to the gallows, because "he would do anything to have the torture stopped."

The vast bulk of the ruling was devoted to recounting Wan's story in all its ugliness; relatively little was devoted to analysis or interpretation. At the end, Brandeis drew the simple conclusion that Wan's confession could not possibly have been voluntary and hence should have been excluded; he distilled the issue into a basic principle:

The Court of Appeals appears to have held the prisoner's statements admissible on the ground that a confession made by one

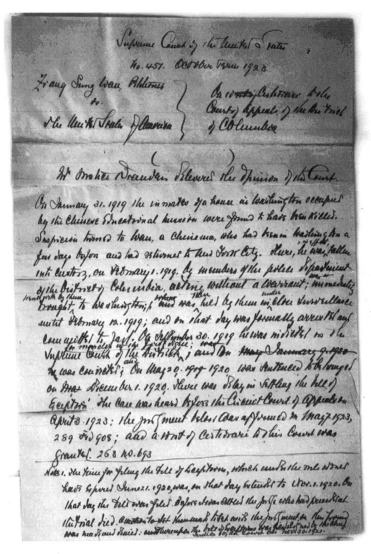

FIG. 22. An early draft of the first page of the *Ziang Sung Wan v. United States* Supreme Court decision in Justice Louis D. Brandeis's handwriting. Source: National Archives and Records Administration.

competent to act is to be deemed voluntary, as a matter of law, if it was not induced by a promise or a threat, and that here there was evidence sufficient to justify a finding of fact that these statements were not so induced. In the federal courts, the requisite of voluntariness is not satisfied by establishing merely that the confession was not induced by a promise or a threat. A confession is voluntary in law if, and only if, it was, in fact, voluntarily made. A confession may have been given voluntarily, although it was made to police officers, while in custody, and in answer to an examination conducted by them. But a confession obtained by compulsion must be excluded whatever may have been the character of the compulsion, and whether the compulsion was applied in a judicial proceeding or otherwise.

The power and seminal nature of the *Wan* decision can be found in its elegance and brevity. It was a clear rebuke to the view that disallowed coerced confessions because they were unreliable. Brandeis decisively advanced the "totality of circumstances" standard and rejected the "no threats or promises" test employed by the lower courts as too narrow. In this sense, it represented a major step forward. The decisions that followed it would be concerned not with repudiating it but with trying to make it work.

Attorney William Cullen Dennis immediately telephoned Wan at the jail to tell him the news. Then he and Van went there to see him. Wan, of course, was thrilled. The first to congratulate him was Eddie Perrygo, a fellow occupant of "gallows lane" scheduled for execution for a 1920 murder to which he had confessed on the day of his arrest. Not coincidentally, Perrygo had also been interrogated by Inspector Grant, tried by Judge Gould, and represented by James A. O'Shea, who had also unsuccessfully opposed the admission of *his* confession, claiming it had been "wrung from him" after he had been denied rest. Perrygo may well have been the second beneficiary of the Supreme Court's decision in the *Wan* case. In less than a month, as a direct result of the ruling, he would be granted a new trial on the grounds that his confession, too, had been involuntary. He would later be permitted to plead to second-degree murder and was sentenced to fifteen additional years in jail but escaped hanging.[17]

The only immediate effect of the ruling was felt at the jailhouse that very night, when death row lost an inmate. Wan was moved back to another part of the prison where, as the *Washington Daily*

News put it, "men live on hope instead of despair." He had been a model prisoner throughout his five years in confinement and would henceforth be given special privileges in return for good behavior. The *News* also tallied all of his stays of execution and noted that the decision marked the *thirteenth* time he had been "snatched . . . from the shadow of the hangman's noose."[18]

Washington police took predictable umbrage at the decision. After all, they had never imagined they were overstepping their bounds until U.S. Attorney Laskey raised the issue before the first trial. Inspector Grant and Detective Kelly both denied that Wan had been coerced; Grant went so far as to assert that he and his colleagues were "very sorry" Wan was to be given a new trial. Grant's boss, Superintendent Daniel Sullivan, asserted that "we do not extort confession by torture" and "we do not stand for any browbeating." Commissioner James F. Oyster, who had been given oversight of the department two years after Wan's interrogation, was less certain. He announced the next day that he intended to launch a thorough investigation of the methods used by the detectives in the *Wan* case. But it was a short-lived effort; five days later, after conferring with Grant, he stubbornly concluded that his men had behaved appropriately.[19]

Police departments throughout the nation also found the decision troubling, but the overall public reaction was extremely positive. "There will be general approval—which Supreme Court decisions do not always get—with the decision in which the Justices this week condemned a confession obtained by what they call duress," the *New York Times* editorialized. "The 'third degree' is more than a myth or a legend," it went on to say. "Often falsely asserted by criminals, they do not always lie about it, and the courts as yet have succeeded only in diminishing the practice of the old, old process of making men talk to their own undoing."[20]

The *New York Sun* hailed the ruling as "a service to the law and the public," noting that "whatever the merits of the case, the decision must be applauded. It constitutes a criticism not of evidence, but of a method of getting evidence . . . The 'third degree' is to be condemned in any case. From its coarser forms of abusive language, threats and blows to the more subtle but no less barbarous examination of a witness beyond the point of reasonable physical endurance, it is a thoroughly uncivilized procedure."[21]

The *Pittsburgh Press* wrote, "The court has plainly and bluntly decided that torture has no place in American legal procedure and that confession thus compelled and extorted may not be admitted as evidence against the accused . . . The 'third degree' is torture of the most cruel nature. In addition, it is direct and wanton violation of all the safeguards of the law that are vouchsafed an accused person."[22]

"Such methods are not reserved for defenseless Chinese. They are what any of us may expect if we are so luckless as to be accused of a crime. Are all of our rights to be abrogated the moment some detective with a conviction to secure puts his hand on our shoulder?" the *New York World* asked. "Where is our security if we can be thus tortured, framed and railroaded to prison or the gallows? . . . It is time the police realized that a man is presumed innocent until proven guilty, and that it is up to them, not the accused himself, to do the proving."[23]

Harvard Law School professor Zechariah Chafee Jr., a well-regarded civil rights advocate, weighed in the following month in an essay in the *New Republic* that appeared together with the text of the decision. Chafee noted the importance of the case "for enforcement of the guarantees of personal liberty" but also praised the opinion for the "powerful light which it casts upon the working of the so-called 'third degree.'" Chafee characterized Justice Brandeis's description of the third degree as the first of its kind by a judge on account of its richness and detail. And he placed the description more broadly among a small but growing public accounting of police abuses across the nation.

Although Chafee believed it "very probable" that Ziang Sung Wan had been justly convicted, he still supported the decision. Foreshadowing arguments that would later transform American police procedures, he explained why coercive police interrogation practices needed to be curtailed. "The most obvious reason," he wrote, was the likelihood that police compulsion would lead to false confessions. But he also feared the deleterious consequences to the police themselves if they relied on coercion. Police, Chafee warned, "will be tempted to rely almost exclusively on this dubious kind of evidence instead of exerting themselves to build up a strong case by searching laboriously for independent proof." Finally, citing the "injurious effect upon the public," Chafee concluded that the rule of law itself would suffer by the use of such police practices. "It is not enough that the people should get justice," he wrote, "They must believe that they are getting justice."

Chafee ended his essay with a plea for an inquiry into "the extent to which the 'third degree' prevails in American cities and a careful consideration of the circumstances under which interrogation of the accused by government officials should be permitted, if at all." In this he was prescient. Such an investigation would indeed take place but not for several more years; he would personally play a major role in it.[24]

One thing the follow-up coverage made clear was that Wan's was no isolated case. The third degree, and police abuse of prisoners more broadly, remained a widespread problem, which surely accounts in part for the decision by the Supreme Court to accept the case in the first place. Many such cases involved abject torture, which of course Wan's case did not.

Locally the *Washington Daily News* cited the recent cases of Arthur A. Davis, a Georgetown blacksmith accused of assault and battery, who alleged that six Washington DC policemen had beaten him with blackjacks and nightsticks in the station house, and of Littleton Poole, allegedly whipped by three Montgomery County, Maryland, officers to get him to confess to the rape of a fourteen-year-old girl.[25] And in an article entitled "Do Washington Police Use the Third Degree?" the same newspaper revisited the case of Aaron Trachtenberg, tried on a narcotics charge in 1922, who had alleged that police had broken his hand, pulled a handful of his hair out by the roots, and beaten him during his interrogation while he was manacled, necessitating ten days in the hospital. It also raised the case of the murder of policeman John W. Purcell, in which the confessions of two defendants had been ruled inadmissible because they had been beaten, one into unconsciousness, by police.[26]

The Supreme Court had not freed Wan; it had merely instructed the lower court to retry him without admitting the confession into evidence. But there was much speculation as to whether there would indeed ever be another trial. The papers were quick to note that in the nearly five years since Wan's conviction, two of the witnesses, including Major Pullman, the chief of police, had died. And there was much public sympathy for the young Chinese. But the decision as to whether to go forward was in the hands of the Justice Department. U.S. Attorney Peyton Gordon struck an agreement with attorney McKenney that no request for action by the Supreme Court of the District of Columbia—the original trial court—would be made until October 27. Gordon wanted to use the intervening weeks to examine the record before deciding on his next step. In the meantime, the District court, anticipating receipt of the paperwork from the Supreme Court, granted Wan an indefinite stay of execution.[27]

"I am inclined to think that Wan will never be brought to trial again," Dennis wrote to Rev. O'Callaghan and others late on the day of the decision. The *Washington Post* thought so too.

They could not have been more wrong.[28]

11

Retrial

IN MUCH OF the press coverage that followed the Supreme Court decision, attorney John W. Davis was lauded as Wan's savior. The *Brooklyn Daily Eagle* ran an article under the headline, "Davis Intervention Saves a Chinese." And the *New York Times* gushed at how Davis, even on a European trip during which he was entertained by the king and queen of England, had kept the case in the forefront of his mind and hurried home to sign the writ of certiorari.[1]

It was only natural for the papers to focus on Davis's contribution; he was, after all, slated to stand for national election in a matter of weeks and he made excellent copy. But while Davis had added marquee value, he had actually done little beyond that.

"To be frank with you," he had written William Cullen Dennis in late 1923, "I have never had time to go into this case with any care, but I am willing to follow you and Mr. McKenney in the matter, and if you choose you may enter my appearance and put my name on the petition for certiorari." And as plans for the oral arguments were taking shape, he had written McKenney, "It was not my understanding when I agreed to participate in the petition for certiorari that I was also to take part in the argument, but if you think the duties of charity are not exhausted, I will endeavor to arrange to do so." He did not ultimately appear however, and, once the Supreme Court had ruled, did not participate further in the case.[2]

The *Times* erred in reporting that the case had been argued by attorneys Dennis and Fahy; Dennis had actually appeared with McKenney. The latter made no reference to the mistake in a subsequent letter to Fahy but the error and the focus on Davis bothered Dennis—who, with Fahy, had done most of the work on the case—and he wrote

Fahy to say so: "There is honor enough to go around, and I shall try to do something in a small way to see that you and Mr. McKenney get some of it."[3]

But there were far worse frictions in the air than any resentments about where credit was due. For some reason, during the course of the Supreme Court's consideration of his case, Wan had soured on James A. O'Shea and was considering firing him. It is not clear why. Because Fahy was not in good health and had retreated to North Carolina for some rest and because neither Dennis, who lacked criminal trial experience, nor McKenney, who was too busy, relished taking the lead chair, significant changes would need to be made to Wan's defense team if a second trial were to occur. Jettisoning O'Shea, who had quarterbacked the effort since the very beginning, would make the transition that much more problematic.[4]

October 27 came and went without any clear indication from U.S. Attorney Gordon as to whether he wished to continue to prosecute Wan, leaving the defense team uncertain as to when to file for speedy action on the Supreme Court's mandate. Dennis drafted such a motion in consultation with McKenney but all felt a decision on Wan's defense team should come first. If the court decided to expedite the trial, the new team would need to be ready.[5]

Dennis urged Wan to consult Father O'Callaghan before taking any precipitous action but by mid-November the prisoner had made up his mind. He wrote O'Shea politely that he would no longer need his services, even though no new attorneys had yet signed up, nor did Wan have the money to retain them. When the matter hit the newspapers on November 25, however, it was framed as a resignation. The report read simply that Wan's attorneys—O'Shea and his colleague John I. Sacks—had withdrawn from the case. No reason was given.[6]

The timing of Wan's dismissal of O'Shea made Dennis's negotiations on his behalf with potential new attorneys more difficult. Some of the lawyers were not interested in working without compensation but at least one was hesitant because he felt O'Shea had gotten a "raw deal." In the end, Father O'Callaghan was summoned to Washington; it was he who persuaded Wilton J. Lambert, one of the most prominent trial lawyers in the country, to take the case without fee.[7]

A Princeton graduate and the latest in a long line of family law-yers, the boyish-looking Lambert had studied law at Georgetown and become a member of the DC bar in 1895 and the Supreme Court bar in 1903. Although his practice consisted primarily of corporate work, he had also handled prominent libel suits and fraud cases. Lambert was no stranger to the Chinese murder case; at the request of the Chinese Legation, he had represented the Munsey Trust Company in 1919 when it petitioned for letters of administration to enable the heirs of Theodore Wong, Chang Hsi Hsie, and Ben Sen Wu to claim their assets. Securing his services free of charge was a coup on O'Callaghan's part. Lambert, however, did not finally agree to sign on until May 1925.[8]

By the end of November the Justice Department had decided to go forward with a second trial. The first order of business of the U.S. attorney's staff was to determine which witnesses would be available to testify. The prosecution's list in 1919 had included fifty-five people, of whom three—all from the police department, Major Raymond W. Pullman among them—were now deceased. Several of the Chinese who had appeared had returned to China, including Dr. Kang Li, who was so vital to the case that he would need to be brought back if there was to be any hope of conviction. Gordon sought the help of the State Department and the Chinese Legation to locate him.

Other witnesses were no longer at their old addresses; to find them, Gordon wrote Attorney General Harlan F. Stone, asking for help from the Bureau of Investigation. His plea was referred to the Bureau, where the newly appointed director, J. Edgar Hoover, signed off on it.[9]

Wan had seen nine condemned men hanged in the years he had been in jail, all the time wondering if he would be next, he wrote later. That question was put to rest shortly after January 22, 1925, when Herbert Copeland, a black man convicted of killing a policeman, died on the gallows. He turned out to be the last person ever hanged for a capital crime in the District of Columbia. Eight days later, President Calvin Coolidge signed a bill that abolished execution by hang-ing in Washington forever.

Within two weeks, the gallows that had served for forty-five years and seen the demise of fifty-three felons was dismantled and burned.

In its place, an electric chair—a means of execution already widely adopted elsewhere in the country—was to be installed. Wan could now take cold comfort in the knowledge that, if retrial resulted in another conviction, he would die with 2,100 volts of electricity coursing through his veins rather than a noose around his neck.[10]

U.S. Attorney Gordon shared Wan's attorneys' worry that the new trial might begin before they were fully prepared for it, but for entirely different reasons. He needed Kang Li desperately; in March 1925 he pressured the State Department to move more quickly to locate and recruit him:

> I am urged by counsel representing Wan to re-set the case for trial, and I am threatened with a motion to that end together with a request that the prisoner be admitted to bail. I am apprehensive of the embarrassment attendant upon such motions and of the result from the showing that could be made as to the long period of imprisonment, and the five months elapsed since the decision of the Supreme Court, especially as I am not in a position to give an approximate date when we could be prepared to go to trial.[11]

The Supreme Court of the District of Columbia did not schedule the case before its summer recess so everyone expected it to be heard in the fall, but even then there was a delay. Kang Li did not arrive until October. The trial was then finally set for January 11, 1926—six years and two days from the date Wan had been pronounced guilty.

Judge Wendell P. Stafford, a former congressman appointed to the bench by President Theodore Roosevelt in 1904, would hear the case; U.S. Attorney Gordon and Assistant U.S. Attorney George D. Horning Jr., a Georgetown graduate formerly attached to the American Legation in the Hague, would appear for the government. Lambert, who now headed the defense team, recruited former Kentucky senator A. Owsley Stanley as associate counsel. A progressive and a Democrat well known for his oratorical skills, he had been a member of the Senate's District of Columbia Committee, where he had spoken out against the use of the third degree in the District as early as 1922, calling it "illegal, vicious and a blot on civilization."[12]

Other members of the team included Lambert's partner, Rudolph

FIG. 23. Judge Wendell P. Stafford.
Source: Library of Congress, LC-H25-105830-G.

H. Yeatman, and his son, Arthur G. Lambert, who had studied law at Harvard but not yet earned his degree. Lambert also cabled an ailing Fahy in New Mexico in early January, asking him to return to Washington to assist. These were the men who would shepherd Wan's case through its final phase in the American judicial system.[13]

With help from Hoover's Bureau of Investigation, the prosecutors were able to cobble together a new list of fifty-five witnesses, although they were impeded by the disappearance of one who had testified in the first trial and the deaths of five others, now including Detective Grant, who had collapsed at his desk the previous month. And during the voir dire process came the news that two more witnesses—a police detective and the night clerk at the Harris Hotel—had passed away, posing a further challenge to the prosecution.[14]

Because seven years had elapsed since the murders, few potential jurors remembered the facts of the case. The key issue in jury selection this time was no longer the use of the third degree but rather attitudes toward convicting on a capital offense based on circumstantial evidence. Many reported opposition to capital punishment under *any* circumstances. The defense naturally also asked about any prejudices against Chinese. As a result, jury selection took nearly four days.[15]

Not only was every seat in the courtroom taken when the trial opened; a line of disappointed spectators spilled out into the corridor. More than twenty Chinese were present, an unusual sight in the courthouse. Father O'Callaghan occupied a place in the front row. Wan, now more mature and substantially stouter than the young man who had been tried there so many years before—he had weighed 109 pounds at the time of his arrest and now tipped the scale at 162—sat with his attorneys, neatly attired in a blue serge suit, a white shirt, and black tie.[16]

The first contentious issue that emerged was that the shorthand notes taken by court reporters at Wan's first trial had all been destroyed. A typewritten transcript survived. The prosecution had intended to use it as a means for the jury to hear from the deceased witnesses, but the defense, sensing an important opportunity, made a determined effort to have all such testimony stricken because the official shorthand notes were no longer available for verifying the transcript.

After several conferences with the judge, the prosecutors were eventually allowed to introduce the transcribed testimony of two witnesses from the first trial, with the stipulation that the defense would be permitted to object to certain portions of it. The first witness was the Chinese man who had introduced Wan to the U.S. Mortgage and Trust Company in 1918, whom the Bureau of Investigation had been unable to locate. He had most likely returned to China but they needed

FIG. 24. A cartoonist depicted the opening day of Wan's second trial.
Source: Library of Congress.

his testimony to establish Wan's financial situation, since they were arguing that money had been Wan's motive for the murder. The second witness was the deceased clerk at the Harris Hotel, where Wan had stayed after he had left the mission. His testimony was required to help place Wan in Washington at the time of the murder.[17]

On January 20 the prosecution introduced a surprise witness with new information that had not come out in the earlier trial. James T. Snead, a handyman who had done odd jobs at the Chinese mission, testified that on the afternoon of January 27, 1919—the day Wan left for the Harris Hotel—Wan had come to the window of the mission and told him he would not need to tend the furnace for several days, since everyone there was going to New York. This suggested that Wan had already planned the murder two days before it was committed.[18]

Next the jury heard from Kang Li, the government's star witness. His testimony was substantially the same as it had been in the first trial: he placed Wan at the crime scene on the day of the murders. Lambert was aggressive in his cross-examination and managed to get Li agitated. But he seemed more interested in pointing out small inconsistencies with what Li had said at the earlier trial than he was in suggesting that Li himself had been the murderer, as O'Shea had done the last time. He was largely ineffective in neutralizing Li's testimony; however, two subsequent witnesses, including Detective—now Captain—Burlingame, did contradict Li in small but not significant ways.

FIG. 25. Dr. Kang Li. Source: *Washington Herald.*

Many witnesses reprised their testimony from the earlier trial. There was some drama when Burlingame was enjoined from speaking about his search of Wan's person and his premises in New York, since these had been accomplished without benefit of a warrant. But the real surprise would come on February 4, when Van took the stand in his brother's defense.

First, however, the jury heard from Wan himself. Wan was palpably tense—so much so that the judge exhorted him not to be nervous and to take his time answering the questions in his own way. Seated beneath a portrait of the late Judge Gould, who had sentenced him to death, he was soft-spoken and almost inaudible. At times jurors had to lean forward to hear him. After reciting his life story, he rebutted the testimony of the handyman, insisting he had never met the man before and was not at the mission on the afternoon their conversation had allegedly taken place. He did not contradict Kang Li's assertion that he had returned on the day of the murder but stated simply that he had left the building shortly after he had seen Li that day.[19]

Van testified after his brother. In the face of withering cross-examination by the prosecution, he clung insistently to his story about T. P. Wong, the strange Chinese man who had allegedly put him up to presenting the check at Riggs Bank, which had always been a weak link in the case. This time, however, the defense dramatically produced a photograph that Van identified as that of T. P. Wong; he had seen it in a newspaper, he said, about three months after the first trial. It was a picture of David Lee Nong, a Chinese man from Binghamton, New York, who had been in the news after his marriage to a twelve-year-old white girl allegedly sold to him by her mother. Nong had since died and would thus conveniently not be available to appear.[20]

Six and a half hours were allotted for closing arguments, which began on February 8. Assistant U.S. Attorney George D. Horning Jr. painted Wan as a man whose greed had driven him to commit cold-blooded murder. But to former senator A. Owsley Stanley, one of Wan's defense counsels, he was an innocent man who had been greatly wronged. "It would have been morally and physically impossible for that broken, emaciated man to have committed the crime with which he is charged," asserted Stanley, whose summation, the *Washington Post* wrote, was "one of the most eloquent ever heard in a local court."

FIG. 26. Attorneys A. Owsley Stanley (*left*) and Wilton J. Lambert (*center*) at trial with Ziang Sung Wan. Courtesy of Roy Delbyk.

The *Post* described how Stanley stood so close to the jury box that his legs brushed against those of a juror. "Did he kill the companion of his youth, the boy who had shown him only kindness and generosity?" he demanded dramatically as he turned to the defendant. "Do you believe it? *Can* you believe it? Was he a fiend and a monster? You may search the stories of Poe and other weird stories, but you will find nothing so strange as this."

Stanley also pointed out that the autopsy on Dr. Wong's body showed he had taken no food for three hours before his death, which meant he had been killed between midnight and 1:00 a.m., whereas the government's own witnesses had placed Wan back at the Harris Hotel at 12:30 a.m.[21]

After receiving instructions from the judge, the jury retired at 3:00 p.m. on February 9. The following morning the twelve men—eleven white and one black—were unable to arrive at consensus and asked the judge to review their instructions. They then returned to the jury room and resumed deliberations. But later that afternoon, after more than twenty-four hours in total, eyes bloodshot and chins dark with stubble, they emerged with the news that they were irretrievably deadlocked and were discharged.

They had voted 10–2 for acquittal.

Wan had been so confident of exoneration that he had packed his belongings before being taken to the courthouse. But he accepted the lack of a verdict with equanimity; he told reporters simply that he hoped for a speedy retrial and that he was confident of acquittal, betraying no emotion. Not so Van; he left the courthouse stifling tears.[22]

A new trial was set for April 12. Judge Adolph A. Hoehling Jr., a Harding nominee on the bench since 1921 who had granted one of Wan's thirteen stays of execution, would preside. The rest of the cast of characters would remain unchanged.[23]

The introduction in the second trial of the photo of David Lee Nong, the Binghamton restaurateur whom Van identified as the man who had given him the check, had so unnerved the prosecutors that they took pains to investigate him. Gordon and Horning traveled to Binghamton the week before the third trial to confer with local police and to search newspaper files for information about Nong, who had died of stomach cancer in 1922. They were hoping for evidence that placed him in town at the time of the murder and were not disappointed. Nong had paid a local grocery bill in person on that date.[24]

Word got out before the trial began that U.S. Attorney Gordon intended to ask that the jury be sequestered this time, a rumor he denied, noting that it would be far more difficult to empanel a jury under those circumstances. Jury selection, in any event, was its usual ordeal, even though Judge Hoehling made it clear that jurors would *not* be locked up for the duration of the trial, which was expected to take four weeks. Still, voir dire required the examination of more than 600 men over a six-day period. Most of those excused had formed an opinion about the case, were opposed to capital punishment, or were disinclined to give much weight to circumstantial evidence in a capital case.[25]

Once the trial began, Lambert elicited the ire of government counsel by deliberately mispronouncing the surname of Kang Li—he said it as "lie" rather than "lee." It so unnerved Horning that he asked the judge to order Lambert to pronounce it properly, something the judge declined to do.[26]

To carry out the order of the Supreme Court to the letter, Judge Hoehling established a timeline for governing the introduction of statements made by Wan while in police custody. Noting that Wan had voluntarily accompanied the police to Washington, he allowed anything Wan said at that time or on the train—up to the time he first asked to be freed, which had occurred while Major Pullman was interrogating him at the Board of Police Surgeons clinic on Fifteenth Street. Nothing he said after that time would be admissible.

Although the third trial proceeded more or less along the same lines as the second, there were some anomalies. Lambert caught Captain Burlingame in some minor inconsistencies in his testimony, while Horning got Kang Li to admit that he had been attending parties with members of the U.S. attorney's office staff since his arrival from China, suggesting he was in their pocket and had been brought to America to do their bidding. The defense also made much of the fact that Li had asked Wan to sign his name in his notebook while they were on the train to Washington, before the police knew about the check forgery, the implication being that Li might have had some knowledge of it.[27]

A government witness, the bellboy from the Harris Hotel, acknowledged that Wan had returned to the hotel on the night of the murder around 11:30 p.m., which Lambert noted made it impossible for Wan to have killed Theodore Wong, who did not arrive home until about 11:00.[28]

Lambert's strategy was to sow reasonable doubt—the standard of proof in criminal cases—by poking holes in the government's case. He set out to demonstrate that the crime took feats of strength of which an ailing, emaciated Wan would have been incapable and that, given the probable time of death based on the coroner's assessment of when Dr. Wong had last taken food, Wan essentially had an alibi.[29] The defense team also put up their own handwriting expert to counter the testimony of the government's authority, who asserted that Wan had forged T. T. Wong's signature on the check stub.

FIG. 27. Judge Adolph A. Hoehling Jr.
Source: Library of Congress, LC-F8-14370.

The defense also produced a surprise witness, a Union Station porter who recalled seeing Van and Wan sitting together at the station on the day the men returned to New York, and then Wan sitting alone. This gave credence to the brothers' contention that Van had gone to Riggs Bank with someone other than Wan. Finally, they put up character witnesses, including Hugh O'Donnell, to attest to Wan's gentle nature.[30]

The last defense witness testified on May 12 that the police had opened a safe at the mission and found it contained stacks of cash and bonds. No police officer had ever made any mention of the safe in either of the previous trials; the lawyers portrayed it as compelling evidence that money had *not* been the motive of whoever had committed the crime.[31]

After six hours of closing arguments—the *Washington Post* reported that men and women "wept unashamedly" during Senator Stanley's plaintive summation—the jurors were given the case at 4:45 p.m. When there was no verdict by 10:00 p.m., the judge locked them up for the night. Wan was taken back to the jailhouse, where he was consoled by Father O'Callaghan.[32]

Twenty-four hours after they had retired, the jurymen were brought back to court. They looked exhausted and grim and reported that they were deadlocked. The judge asked if there were any matters of law he might explain to assist in their deliberations but the law was not the issue. The foreman asserted that they were "utterly and everlastingly in disagreement."

U.S. Attorney Gordon then asked that the jury be discharged, a suggestion that met with fierce protest from Lambert. But eventually the judge relented: at 10:00 p.m. on May 13 he dismissed the jurors. This time the vote had been nine for acquittal, three for conviction.

Lambert seized the opportunity to ask the judge to set bail for Wan. "It would be inhuman to incarcerate this man any longer," he asserted. "He has been in jail for seven and a half years. Twenty-four men have considered the case." But the judge made no immediate ruling on the request, nor on the formal motion for bond that Lambert filed the next week. Wan, who had appeared crestfallen as he left the courtroom, maintained that he didn't much care whether he stayed in jail or not.

Major Gordon declined to comment on whether there would be a fourth trial, though Horning asserted in front of a large crowd that there would. The expectation in most quarters was that, absent a verdict in the third trial, the case would now be "nolle prossed"—that is, the charges would be dismissed. When two weeks passed after the discharge of the jury without a decision on a fourth trial, Lam-

FIG. 28. From left, Ziang Sung Wan, attorney Wilton J. Lambert, and Tsong Ing Van outside the District of Columbia Courthouse on June 16, 1926, after all charges against Wan were dropped. Source: collection of the author.

bert decided to ask Judge Hoehling to dismiss the case, although he knew such a move would be unlikely.[33]

On May 27, as part of his formal motion, Lambert submitted affidavits from all nineteen of the jurors who had favored acquittal, reiterating their belief in Wan's innocence and asking that he be set free. Gordon preempted the proceedings and announced that, in consultation with his superiors, he would decide on a course of action "within the next few weeks." Since an immediate retrial was impossible, however, a fourth trial would have to wait until the court's October term.[34]

It took until June 5 for Major Gordon's boss, Attorney-General John G. Sargent, a Republican nominated by President Calvin Coolidge, to conclude that, without Wan's confession, the government was unlikely ever to see him convicted for murder and that further proceedings would just be a waste of taxpayers' money. The three trials had already cost the government an estimated $150,000—about $2 million in today's dollars. Gordon announced that he intended to go before

Judge Hoehling on June 16, not to exonerate Wan but to withdraw the charges against him.[35]

That morning, the courtroom was packed. Aisles were jammed, doorways blocked, and spectators were even perched on windowsills. They did not expect suspense or drama so much as they wished to witness a historic moment. When Major Gordon rose to address Judge Hoehling at 10:05 a.m., he did not admit that the government's case was a failure. He noted that key witnesses had died and returned to China and that the government was unable to produce additional evidence of Wan's guilt. He then stated his belief that no jury could be obtained "which would render a verdict either of guilty or not guilty" and requested that, under the circumstances, the judge nolle pros all charges against him.

At the same time, he requested that the court order that the uttering charge against Tsong Ing Van be dropped as well. With no actual check to introduce as evidence, the government's chance of securing a conviction in that case seemed equally small, if not smaller.

Three minutes later, with what the *Washington Post* called a "benign smile," Judge Hoehling asked Wan to rise from his seat at the counsel table. As he stood on the very same spot in the very same courtroom in which he had been condemned more than six years earlier to be "hanged by the neck" until he was dead, he heard the judge order the indictments against both him and his brother dismissed.

Ziang Sung Wan was a free man.[36]

One by one, the attorneys pumped Wan's hand and a crowd soon formed around him. A bailiff was able to extricate him from the press of well-wishers and escort him back to the holding cell, where he had left his hat. But when he emerged from the courthouse to pose for photographs, he was mobbed once again. From there, the longest-serving inmate in the history of the District of Columbia Jail—he had spent seven years and 125 days in confinement there—headed back one last time to pick up his belongings and say his goodbyes.

From the jail he was squired away to attorney Lambert's office in the Munsey Building at 1329 E. Street NW, where they sent a telegram to Father O'Callaghan, who was at a conference in Chicago. The final order of business for the day was a sumptuous meal at a fine local restaurant. It was Wan's first steak—and the first meal he was able to eat with a knife and fork—since he had entered prison.

Wan had prepared a typewritten statement to release to the press following the withdrawal of charges. It included a sentence hinting at his desire to clear his name:

> I feel deeply grateful to the public and the press for many expressions of confidence and support. Not one of the three trials brought out clearly the real facts of my case. "Rules of evidence" in your law courts seem designed to cover up instead of uncover actual facts, and so it has happened that many facts which if fully understood would, I believe, have exonerated me completely, and long ago, could not be developed, and in some instances were not even touched upon.[37]

But Wan himself had already hatched plans to set the record straight as to the facts of his case. It was one of the items on his to-do list as he walked out into the sunlight.

12

Freedom

WITHIN A DAY of Wan's release, some "friends of Wan" began talking about incorporating the lessons of his case into a broader national discussion of problems in the criminal justice system. "No remedial action or redress is sought on Wan's behalf," the *Evening Star* asserted, without identifying any of these friends. "What is desired is to make his amazing fortune the peg on which can be hung an investigation of what's wrong with American criminal procedure."

The *Star* went on to point out that some of the best-known legal figures in the country had been associated with Wan's case, suggesting that "undoubtedly they would be lent to any movement designed to make the young Chinese [*sic*] fate the basis for reform in procedure." It predicted that, now that Wan was at liberty, figures such as Davis, McKenney, Stanley, and Dennis would join in such an effort.[1]

Apart from the issue of the third degree, there were other lessons these friends wished to draw from the *Wan* case. "The law, as it does in some states, should put a limit on the number of times a person may be tried for the same offense," the *New York Times* quoted one of Wan's attorneys as saying. "The law should also permit judges to *nolle pros* cases on their own initiative. In the Federal courts, criminal charges can be dismissed only on the motion of the prosecution, which always is the Department of Justice. There should be speedier procedures in handling appeals. There is no logical reason why a person should be kept in jail more than seven years awaiting a final disposition of a charge against him."[2]

Wan's prolonged incarceration had been the result not of a conspiracy so much as a string of misfortunes. The fact that it took four full months for the case to reach the grand jury and another three for the body to issue indictments in 1919—resulting in the first trial being delayed until nearly a year after the murders—was due to U.S. Attorney Laskey's concern about the admissibility of Wan's confession and his desire for more evidence from the police. The fact that Wan's appeal was not heard until more than three years after his conviction was a function of quarreling between the prosecution and the defense over the contents of the bill of exceptions, the death of the trial judge, and then the desire of Wan's attorneys to use the death as a pretext for a new trial.

The Supreme Court had granted the writ of certiorari in October 1923 but did not hear oral arguments until April of the following year because of attorney Dennis's foreign travel and the tardiness of Wan's legal team in preparing its brief. The combination of the late date and Justice Brandeis's deliberate approach did not permit the preparation and issuance of an opinion until the following October. And the fact that Wan's second and third trials did not take place until more than a year after the court acted was due to the difficulty of locating witnesses so many years after the murders and the fact that one had to be brought back from China.

The "friends of Wan" had a couple of vehicles in mind for considering the issues raised by his ordeal. The first was the American Bar Association, whose American Law Institute, under the leadership of now former attorney general George W. Wickersham, was in the process of drafting a model criminal code for general adoption. The organization was due to hold its annual meeting in Denver in mid-July; Wan's friends hoped to get these questions on the agenda for the planned discussion of criminal law procedure.

The model code, which took several years to complete, included recommendations such as relaxing the unanimity requirement for jury verdicts for non-capital offenses, permitting questioning by a presiding judge, giving appellate courts power to pass on the merits of a case as well as the law, and naming extra jury members as insurance against mistrials through juror death or incapacity. Parts of the code were ultimately adopted by several states. Although it is arguable whether one or more of its provisions might have benefitted Wan had they been enshrined in law during his lengthy ordeal, it does not appear to have dealt with the central issue of his case, namely, the methods employed to elicit his confession.[3]

The second organization Wan's "friends" hoped to engage was a body appointed by President Calvin Coolidge the previous year called the National Crime Commission. It included such luminaries as former secretary of state (and future Supreme Court justice) Charles Evans Hughes, former secretary of war Newton D. Baker, and former assistant secretary of the navy Franklin D. Roosevelt.

The very existence of a national commission was an indication that crime was becoming a bigger problem for the federal government. It had always been primarily a state-level concern, but Prohibition, which took effect in 1920, had made the production and sale of alcoholic beverages federal offenses. Together with the Harrison Narcotics Tax Act of 1914, which regulated the manufacture, distribution, and importation of drugs, and the Mann Act, passed in 1910 to outlaw transportation across state lines of women for the purposes of prostitution, the Eighteenth Amendment had greatly expanded the federal government's role in law enforcement in the first two decades of the century.

The National Crime Commission was not notably effective; it did not even establish the existence of a national crime wave in the country at the time. And it did not specifically take up the lessons of the case of Ziang Sung Wan. But these would be considered a few years later by a successor committee.[4]

For his part, Wan was concerned far less with reforming the legal system that had victimized him than with restoring his good name. In a series of exclusive articles published under his byline in the *Washington Times* that ran for more than two weeks between July 21 and August 7, Wan told his story, his way. He had likely drafted the pieces during his incarceration and may have been paid for them.

"I would like it clearly understood," he wrote at the outset, "that I am not writing for the purpose of gaining sympathy, but only for understanding." And he proceeded to parse the narrative of his case, pointing out inconsistencies and offering alternate explanations.

Like his attorneys, Wan attempted to poke holes in the government's case—and there were many such gaps. It was certainly true that once the detectives had set their sights on him, they had not seriously pursued any other suspects or scenarios; Wan made the most of this. "From all this evidence, which has so slowly come to light and which indicates still more not yet uncovered," he wrote, "I know that I was not arrested and jailed because of any honest mistake on the part of the authorities, but because they either wanted the glory of solving a Chinese murder mystery, which all police circles know to be 99 percent unsolvable, or because the temptation to secure the reward offered by the Chinese government was too much to resist." (There is, however, no record of any reward offered or paid by the Chinese Legation.) He also accused the government of destroying evidence that did not support its case against him.[5]

Although he claimed he wished only to suggest other avenues the police might have pursued, he clearly intended to point a finger at Kang Li. "I am not making accusations against anyone and I do not want to do Kang Li an injustice," he wrote, "but it was he who threw suspicion upon me in the first place . . . it therefore is necessary for me to show how an even stronger case of circumstantial evidence could have been built up against Kang Li if the police had cared to follow other clues."[6]

In the service of this goal, he suggested that Li might have been in cahoots with the two men who allegedly talked his brother into attempting to cash the forged check on their behalf. He reminded readers that Li had possessed a key to the mission and disputed Li's contention that he had returned it to Dr. Wong. He noted that Police Detective Charles H. Bradley had testified that the window through which Li had ostensibly entered the mission house had been locked earlier in the day. He pointed out that Li had never been asked on the stand to account for his whereabouts on the night of the murder and that, despite being a physician, he did not attempt to examine the body of Dr. Wong but instead ran into the street at the sight of it. And he noted that it had been Kang Li who had identified the murder weapon, describing it as rusty and hard to operate—something he would have known, Wan suggested, only if he had fired it.[7]

Wan used the last eight installments of the seventeen articles he wrote for the *Times* to deconstruct the actual confession, which he claimed he signed "when I was sick and willing to die, if I could exculpate my brother Van." The paper ran the actual text of the confession and Wan's commentary and analysis side by side. Taken as a whole, the series was an exhaustive manifesto of Wan's considered view of the entire ordeal.

After his release, Wan had headed for Oakland, New Jersey, where he was a guest at Father O'Callaghan's farm. After that he spent several days in Warren, Pennsylvania, at the home of Hiram R. McCalmont, a Civil War veteran whose daughter Mabel planned to write a book about his case. But cooperation with her—which had involved some vague promises of shared profits—soon unraveled. No book was ever published.[8]

Although he was keen to return to China to see his aged mother, Wan had not decided to go home permanently; if he wished to reserve the right to come back to the United States, there was a very practical matter to attend to first. Wan had entered the country as a student in 1916 but had not been at school for many years. As soon as he was released from jail, he was out of status as far as the federal government was concerned and presumably subject to summary deportation. The Chinese Exclusion Act was still in effect in 1926—it would not be repealed until 1943—and that meant that, in order for a Chinese who was not a citizen and who entered after the act was passed to be a legal resident, he or she had to be classified as a diplomat, a scholar, or a merchant, or else an immediate family member of someone who fell into one of those categories.[9]

So Wan decided to go into business, something that would afford him legal status and the opportunity to earn money to pay off debts and purchase a ticket home. Among the privileges he had been granted after he left death row was permission to run a small business within the prison walls. He had chosen to bake pies and sell them to the other prisoners. This permitted him to put away a little cash; it also gave him some experience in food preparation. He had given a lot of thought to nutrition over the years; he credited a diet and exercise program of his own devising for his ability to regain his health and put on weight while incarcerated. And so before the end of the year, he put his knowledge to work and set up a candy business.

WAN'S MANDARIN CREAMS

This candy, made of fresh and pure ingredients, is a most nourishing **FOOD. Chemical** analyses show that the nuts used in my "MANDARIN CREAMS" contain the highest protein and lowest fat content of any nut grown. The following authentic figures tell the story:

	Protein	Fat	Carbohydrates (Sugar & Starches)	Mineral Matter
NUTS used in MANDARIN CREAMS	83.90	48.20	7.90	3.80
Almonds	21.40	54.40	16.80	2.50
Pecans	12.10	70.70	8.50	1.60
Walnuts (English)	18.40	64.40	13.00	1.70

The extraordinary protein content combined with the valuable vitamins of FRESH ORANGES, makes this an ideal confection for the fat person, for invalids and for children.

If you like this, order a weekly delivery for your family, and introduce it to your friends.

Price: $.50 a box $.55 by mail
1.00 large box   1.10 by mail

With best wishes for the Holiday Season,

"MANDARIN CREAMS" for sale at
1705 K Street N. W. (Draper Building)   Telephone: Franklin 1625.

FIG. 29. A circular advertising "Wan's Mandarin Creams."
Source: Library of Congress.

While staying with the McCalmonts, Wan began experimenting with candy making. By May 1927 he had incorporated a confectionery business in Delaware and was operating it at 1424 Park Road NW in Washington DC. His lone product was called "Wan's Mandarin Creams," which sold at a downtown office building for fifty cents a box. The candy was touted as especially nourishing, "an ideal confection for the fat person, the invalid and for children," though it's hard to see the benefit that candy filled with sugar, almonds, pecans, and walnuts would confer on someone who was overweight. The company's authorized capital was $25,000 and its vice president was Mabel McCalmont. Where he got the money to start the business is unclear.

Having established himself as a bona fide merchant, Wan was now in a position to visit China with a guarantee of return to the United States. In September 1928 he was issued a reentry permit by the Immigration Service and was soon off for Shanghai by way of Seattle.

Wan surely enjoyed a reunion with his mother, who had sadly gone blind since his departure so many years earlier. According to him, she had never been told of his troubles during his years of incarceration; the fact that there is no record of her having financed his defense supports this. Theodore Wong's descendants, on the other hand, tell the story of his widow turning away Mrs. Wan when she called at their home in an attempt to apologize and offer compensation for her husband's death. It is not clear when this might have happened or even if it did. By the time Wan returned to Shanghai, he was no longer accused—formally, at least—of any of the three murders.[10]

Wan remained in Shanghai for several months. By March 1929 he was once again back in America but apparently only to wind down his affairs. He is listed in the 1929 Washington DC city directory, but not the 1930 edition; nor is he enumerated in the federal census, which was taken in early April that year. The candy company appears to have gone out of business at about the same time.

Back in Shanghai once again, Wan got on with his life. He never again returned to the country he maintained had so severely wronged him.

13

The Wickersham Report

EVEN AFTER WAN'S release and his return to China, his case continued to have staying power. In 1929 a president's commission saw to it that it once again received national attention as a damning example of police misconduct.

President Calvin Coolidge's 1925 National Crime Commission had not accomplished much and the perception that crime was on the upswing in America had only increased as the decade wore on. The Eighteenth Amendment to the Constitution had rendered illegal the production, distribution, and consumption of alcohol but it hadn't diminished America's taste for it; the world of bootlegging and speakeasies created by Prohibition was providing many avenues for organized crime. Rule of law seemed threatened. People were alarmed.

Although the Republican Herbert Hoover, who favored Prohibition, handily won the presidential election of 1928—Coolidge had declined to run again—public outcry over an epidemic of gang wars in the late 1920s (including Chicago's infamous 1929 St. Valentine's Day massacre, which occurred just over a month before his inauguration) prompted him to order a review of how well the policy was being enforced and to seek recommendations for its improvement. As Hoover told the nation in his March 4 inaugural address, "Justice must not fail because the agencies of enforcement are either delinquent or inefficiently organized. To consider these evils, to find their remedy, is the most sore necessity of our times."[1]

To spearhead this effort, Hoover recruited former attorney general George W. Wickersham, the well-regarded national figure who had served both Democratic and Republican administrations. Pennsylvania-born Wickersham had enforced antitrust laws aggressively while at the Justice Department and helped draft the Sixteenth Amendment, which authorized a federal income tax. During World War I, President Woodrow Wilson had appointed him to the War Trade Board; he had most recently presided over the National Probation Association, which promoted prison reform, and the American Law Institute, which was drafting the new model criminal code. The seventy-one-year-old jurist was an inspired choice to head the new National Commission on Law Observance and Enforcement, which was announced in May 1929 and expected to function for two years.[2]

Although Prohibition was the proximate driver of the establishment of the blue-ribbon body—which immediately became known as the "Wickersham Commission"—Hoover gave the eleven-member group a very broad mandate. He charged it with identifying the causes of criminal activity in the United States and making recommendations for changes in law enforcement.[3]

Among the commissioners were several noted jurists. Former secretary of war Newton D. Baker had chaired Coolidge's earlier National Crime Commission; Roscoe Pound was the dean of Harvard Law School. Max Lowenthal had served on President Wilson's Mediation Committee and Frank J. Loesch was the founder of the Chicago Crime Commission. Monte M. Lemann, president of the Louisiana Bar Association, and Kenneth R. Mackintosh, former chief justice of the Washington State Supreme Court, were joined by federal judges Paul J. McCormick, William S. Kenyon, and William I. Grubb. Also asked to serve was Ada L. Comstock, the president of Radcliffe College, the only woman on the panel. None of the commissioners had previously been identified as "wet" or "dry" or been notably outspoken on the question of Prohibition.

From the outset, Wickersham—who testified before Congress in 1911 that he had "never heard of the use of the so-called 'third degree' by any Federal official"—let it be known that all bodies interested in law enforcement were welcome to submit reports on pertinent issues and that the group intended to convene meetings with representatives of labor organizations, law enforcement bodies, and others. At its first meeting, the commission established two subcommittees, one to investigate the causes of crime and the other to deal with its rem-

FIG. 30. President Herbert Hoover and Attorney General William D. Mitchell pose on the White House lawn with members of the newly created National Commission on Law Observance and Enforcement, known as the Wickersham Commission, May 28, 1929. *Front row, seated, left to right:* Roscoe Pound, Ada L. Comstock, Attorney General Mitchell, President Hoover, Commission Chairman George W. Wickersham, and William S. Kenyon. *Back row, left to right:* Kenneth R. Mackintosh, Monte M. Lemann, Paul J. McCormick, William I. Grubb, Frank J. Loesch, Newton D. Baker, and Henry W. Anderson. Source: Library of Congress, LC-H2-B-3396.

edies. It also announced that it would hold public hearings in various locations around the country.[4]

Unlike its underfunded predecessor, the Wickersham Commission was allotted substantial resources to fulfill its mandate. Its initial budget was $250,000—about $3.4 million in today's dollars—and by the end of its life it had spent nearly twice that amount. This level of funding enabled it to hire professional staff and to engage outside experts in conducting empirical research and drafting the vast bulk of the report language. With such generous support, it was able to produce fourteen separate reports comprising more than 4,000 pages before being disbanded in mid-1931.[5]

The volumes were issued over a seven-month period beginning in January 1931. Only two actually focused on Prohibition. Although they were quite critical of the policy, its costs, and its enforcement, they fell short of calling for its end. This was likely out of deference to the president, who did not favor repeal, as seven out of the eleven commissioners did. The Prohibition reports naturally commanded most of the attention.

The other reports focused on various aspects of criminal justice and ultimately had little long-term impact, save one: Volume XI, *Lawlessness in Law Enforcement*. Conveyed to the president on June 25 and made public in August, it was galvanizing and memorable for its frank and critical assessment of the use of third-degree tactics by law enforcement officers in America.[6]

The principal co-author of 347-page document was Zechariah Chafee Jr., a legal scholar and civil liberties expert who served as one of the commission's outside consultants and who has been described as "the most distinguished guardian of civil rights in the first half of the twentieth century."[7] A New England Brahmin, he had been recommended by Roger N. Baldwin, a founder of the American Civil Liberties Union, which had been especially vocal in the national debate over police misconduct.[8] Chafee was a Harvard Law School professor, though a controversial one: in 1921, he had been branded a radical for his advocacy of free speech during wartime and nearly lost his job, an incident that had earned him an accolade from Supreme Court Justice Brandeis at the time. Chafee's writings on freedom of speech had influenced Brandeis, who quoted them in at least one decision; the men were friends. On the commission report, Chafee worked together with two prominent New York law partners who were fellow civil libertarians: Walter H. Pollak and Carl S. Stern.[9]

Chafee had analyzed and praised the Supreme Court's decision in the *Wan* case in a 1924 *New Republic* essay in which he worried that coercion led to false confessions, encouraged lax police investigations, and undermined the rule of law. He had pleaded in that article for a broad inquiry into the use of the third degree across the country. The Wickersham Commission was a golden opportunity that provided him with a much larger canvas on which to record his conclusions.[10]

The writers had no illusions about the widespread use or the legality of the third degree, which they defined broadly as "the employment of methods which inflict suffering, physical or mental, upon a person, in order to obtain from that person information about a crime." They called it a "secret and illegal practice" that violated several fundamental rights. Violence, the use of force, and physical suffering were not required; it was clear that prolonged and relentless questioning, sleep and food deprivation, and the like were very much included in their definition. So they saw their task as "to lay the facts—the naked, ugly facts—of the existing abuses before the public, in the hope that the pressure of public condemnation may be so aroused that the conduct so violative of the fundamental principles of constitutional liberty . . . may be entirely abandoned."[11]

At the outset of the substantive section of the report, the authors noted the difficulty of getting reliable information about a practice that many denied existed and others greatly exaggerated. They thus began with a statement of methodology. The writers had undertaken a review of literature, adjudicated cases, and appeals briefs, focusing on the period between 1925 and 1930. They had also evaluated existing statutes and studies and scrutinized newspaper accounts. Questionnaires were sent out to public defenders, bar associations, and legal aid societies, among others. And interviews of present and former judges, prosecutors, police commissioners, police chiefs, local American Civil Liberties Union representatives, reporters, law professors, prison wardens, and prisoners were carried out in fifteen cities.[12]

The writers maintained that the use of the third degree—which they found to be widespread but not ubiquitous—conflicted with two basic legal principles. First, that people should not be compelled to furnish evidence against themselves; second, that confessions obtained under duress are not admissible as evidence. That mental, not just physical, suffering was included in this definition was established early in the report by the inclusion of a lengthy quote from Justice Brandeis's opinion in the *Wan* case on the issue of voluntariness. The writers cited several contributory factors, including illegal arrests, the use of excessive force, illegal detention, wrongful denial of bail or habeas corpus, isolation of prisoners from family and friends, denial of counsel, and confinement under substandard conditions.[13]

An assessment of the extent of the use of the third degree in the

FIG. 31. Professor Zechariah Chafee Jr. Source: Historical and Special Collections, Harvard Law School Library.

United States comprised the bulk of the report. Although there was general agreement from nearly everyone consulted that the use of force was illegal, that did not mean it did not occur. Only present and former police officials categorically denied its existence, or at least its severity. The writers quoted a litany of law enforcement officials who blamed the newspapers and "yellow journalism" for defaming what they maintained was essentially a benign set of practices aimed only at seeking the truth. But Chafee and the others rejected these assessments; there was too much evidence to the contrary.

From more than half the states in the nation, the authors gathered example upon example of brutal police misconduct and described, in rich and disturbing detail, many instances of abject torture. They chronicled the inquisition of a Nebraska prisoner who continually denied murdering a penitentiary guard despite being brutally and repeatedly struck in the face with clenched fists. They told of a university professor arrested in Ohio, also for murder, who refused to confess to police, only to be struck in the jaw several times by the county prosecutor himself, even as his lawyer, barred from the interrogation room, pounded on the door demanding admittance. And they recounted the story of a Florida man, accused of murdering his wife, who was chained overnight to the floor of a cell infested with mosquitoes and subsequently interrogated for hours with the scalp of his dead wife perched at his feet.[14]

The commission found that the practice was not used only on suspects; witnesses were also often subjected to it and it was employed most commonly in murder cases. Most victims were young males, not necessarily with previous criminal records; these skewed heavily toward the "poor and uninfluential." Third-degree practices were particularly harsh in the case of minorities. The writers told of an eighteen-year-old black man who was whipped for a week until he confessed to two murders, as well as a 1925 Mississippi murder investigation in which a black man charged with killing a white man was pinned to the floor as water was poured down his nostrils until he nearly drowned—an early instance of waterboarding. And in a 1929 Arkansas case, a black man confessed after being forced into an improvised electric chair and shocked.[15]

Not all the cases employed physical torture, of course. Those that involved harassment of other kinds were more common. Among the non-violent but no less abusive tactics were holding people incom-

municado, without access to counsel; relay questioning; taking prisoners "around the loop," which meant moving them from one police
station to another to lessen the chance of attorneys catching up with
them; and quartering suspects in filthy conditions.

The report cited two Washington DC cases as examples of mental
suffering. The use of the third degree had been proven in the case of
Eddie Perrygo, who had languished on death row in the District of
Columbia jailhouse together with Ziang Sung Wan after succumbing
to prolonged questioning from the same Inspector Grant who had
been one of Wan's interrogators. The same was true of Wan, whose
case, cited for its reliance on sleep deprivation and protracted interrogation, occupied three full pages in the report. It was noted that
Wan's room had been searched without a warrant; that he had been
held incommunicado for eight days; and that he had been questioned
incessantly, despite being extremely ill, in sessions that sometimes
lasted into the wee hours.[16]

In the interest of objectivity, Chafee and the others made a sincere
attempt to give the proponents of the third degree their due. They
considered several arguments, which mostly centered around the
assertion of *necessity*: that the use of the third degree was essential
for getting at the facts of a case, especially when dealing with shrewd
suspects; that it was used only against the guilty, which of course was
a ludicrous claim and certainly not borne out by the facts; that obsta-
cles faced by police made it nearly impossible to obtain convictions
in other ways; that police brutality was an "excusable reaction to the
brutality of criminals"; that restricting the ability of officers to use it
might impair police morale; and that it was justified by the existence
of organized gangs in large cities.

Outweighing these, in the estimation of the authors, were four
specific evils posed to society by the use of the third degree. First
was the ever-present danger of false confession, documented with
many examples. Second was the impairment of police efficiency:
the data showed, it was argued, that excessive reliance on confessions made police less zealous in searching for objective evidence.
Third, the practice was said to introduce a new issue into trials—
whether the police had misbehaved in eliciting the confession, giv-

ing them a strong incentive for committing perjury. It also increased the chances of the guilty being set free. And fourth, they found, the third degree "brutalizes the police, hardens the prisoner against society, and lowers the esteem in which the administration of justice is held by the public."[17]

Chafee, Pollak, and Stern made a creditable case against the third degree in *Lawlessness in Law Enforcement*, but their work was lacking in the anemic section on recommendations—only seven out of 347 pages, shared with the report's conclusions. They called for no sweeping changes, just eleven specific reforms, such as the establishment of a statutory minimum time for the preparation of a defense, the inclusion of qualified persons on jury lists "regardless of their color," and the abolition of the practice of paying judges, prosecutors, and court officials from fines and court costs. Their basic position was that "the law as it stands is sufficient" and that the difficulty was that it was not enforced or was deliberately disobeyed.[18]

Once it became public in August 1931, the report naturally provoked considerable discussion. Although some of the nation's newspapers quibbled with the commission's findings as they related to their own communities, while others remained agnostic as to the veracity of the facts presented, editorial boards were, in the main, sympathetic.

"America wants results from its police, but it wants them according to law," opined the *Dallas Morning News*. "Incommunicado cells in Dallas or any other city are as much an offense against justice as any crime the police are called to combat," it continued. The *Cleveland Plain Dealer* observed: "No civilized community would tolerate what the Wickersham group complains of if the community were aware of it . . . To try to enforce the law by lawless methods is a confession of ineptitude."[19]

North Carolina's *Greensboro Daily News* referred to "this blot of infamy in a supposedly civilized country, which would on occasion do credit to the cruelties of the Spanish Inquisition." The *Trenton Evening Times*, while asserting that "vicious violators of the statutory code do not deserve to be handled with kid gloves," nevertheless insisted that "the alleged criminal should be treated in a civilized manner which is far removed from the fiendishness of an inquisition." The *San Fran-*

cisco Chronicle agreed, asserting, "If there is a grain of truth it is too much." But it quickly added, "San Francisco wants the evidence."[20]

From police departments and prosecutors around the country came predictable denials and rebuttals. Years later, Chafee noted wryly that "our report was greeted by the police with two answers which they regarded as conclusive: first, there wasn't any third degree; and second, they couldn't do their work without it." Chief Thomas F. Daley of the Westfield, Massachusetts Police told the *Springfield Republican*, "I do not believe in it. I will not stand for it." Yet the International Association of Chiefs of Police denounced the report as "the greatest blow to police work in the last half century," while an acting district attorney in New York asked rhetorically, "What are we to do, give our baby killers ice cream sodas?" Others played a defensive game: John H. Alcock, acting commissioner of the Chicago Police Department, said he had ordered it stopped fourteen months earlier, offering to investigate any complaints against any of his men and to dismiss the offenders if proven.[21]

In communities that had played host to specific cases profiled in the report, the papers naturally sought comment from local officials and in general received what one paper called a "burst of denials." But even in communities not mentioned, angry police officials spoke out. For example, Joseph E. Demers, chief of police of Springfield, Massachusetts, told the *Springfield Republican* that the Wickersham Commission should leave the machinery of the law alone and spend its time investigating the "crooks at Washington," whose graft, he assured readers, ran into the millions of dollars.

Because the report had included several references to the *Wan* case, the two police detectives still living who had participated in Wan's grilling were contacted by the local press; both chose to speak out about the case. Edward J. Kelly, now a captain, and Guy E. Burlingame, now a retired captain, both denied that Wan had been ill treated during his interrogation. Kelly asserted that, if Wan had been mistreated, it must have been when he was absent from the room. Burlingame was more categorical: "At no time was Wan abused, threatened or beaten," he told the *Evening Star*, and he had never complained about his treatment. But the *Evening Star* reminded its readers that, when Wan had been brought to Washington, "strenuous efforts were made to conceal that fact" and he had been held incommunicado at the Dewey Hotel.[22]

The Wickersham Commission Report raised the issue of the third degree to national awareness. In shining a bright light on the practice, it pressured police departments around the nation to professionalize their practices and forgo coercive interrogations, the use of which indeed diminished in the decades that followed, though somewhat unevenly.[23] It was not until 1940 that the first police interrogation manual was published in America.[24]

It also set the stage for the Supreme Court to involve itself, as it never had before, in the issue of protection against self-incrimination—and hence in the admissibility of coerced confessions—in state courts.

14

The Road to Miranda

IN ITS RULING in the case of *Ziang Sung Wan v. United States*, the Supreme Court had broken new ground in American criminal justice, reaffirming the principle first stated in *Bram v. United States* that the Fifth Amendment permitted only voluntary confessions to be admitted as evidence in federal proceedings. It had also stated explicitly that excluding only those made in response to promises or threats was simply too narrow a test for voluntariness.

But two additional, important challenges lay ahead before all of America's accused could enjoy full protection under this new principle of law. First, the new standard applied only to cases before the federal courts, where the Constitution indisputably governed. The privileges promised the accused in the Bill of Rights had not yet been determined to apply to the states and localities. This convoluted process, known as the "incorporation doctrine," actually took decades. In *Lawlessness in Law Enforcement*, the Wickersham Commission had pointed out countless examples of coerced confessions on the state and local levels, but it had not specifically discussed, in its paltry list of recommendations, the need to extend the standard articulated in *Wan* beyond the federal system. Many state courts nonetheless took immediate note of the *Wan* decision and cited it to support their use of the voluntariness standard.

Second, the new standard lacked clarity. For all the elegance of its *Wan* decision, the Taft court hadn't really replaced the old test with anything tangible. Brandeis hadn't provided a satisfactory definition of "voluntariness" or instructions on how to ensure it. He had found that "a confession obtained by compulsion must be excluded whatever may have been the character of the compulsion" but he had made no attempt to delimit the ingredients of "compulsion." As a result the concept remained open to interpretation and the standard was inconsistently applied. For all his eloquence, the good justice had left the country with a shining principle that was something of a tautology. As a result, abuses unfortunately continued.

If state judiciaries were to be held to the *Wan* standard, the stage would first have to be set. The Supreme Court would need to step in again, more than once. It opened the door in 1932 in the case of *Powell v. Alabama*. This was the famous case of the "Scottsboro Boys," nine southern black teenagers who had been accused of raping a white woman. The young men, all but one of whom were convicted and sentenced to death in rushed trials that lasted just a day, had been given no advance access to attorneys, nor had they even been told before their trials that they had a right to counsel.

After the Alabama Supreme Court upheld all but one of their convictions, the defendants appealed to the U.S. Supreme Court. In a 7–2 decision, the court ordered new trials, ruling that the "due process clause" of the Fourteenth Amendment—the stipulation that "no person shall be deprived of life, liberty of property without due process of law"—had been violated.[1]

Powell v. Alabama had nothing to do with confessions. It was about fairness and the right to counsel, enshrined in the Sixth Amendment, not the Fifth. But the court decided that it was one of the fundamental rights guaranteed to all by the Constitution and that state courts were every bit as bound to respect it as federal courts. The case was thus a watershed: the ruling marked the first time the Supreme Court had reversed a *state-level* criminal conviction on *constitutional* grounds. It did not guarantee Fifth Amendment rights to state-level defendants but it did find that they were entitled to at least some of the protections of the Sixth Amendment.

It was a beginning.

Four years after *Powell*, another case—also involving black defendants, who were in far more peril than whites of having their rights trampled by the state courts, especially in the Deep South—reached the Supreme Court. *Brown v. Mississippi* was a murder case. Three black tenant farmers accused of killing a white planter had been brutally whipped and one had actually been strung up on a tree, to get them to confess. Their confessions were admitted anyway; as in Wan's case, jurors were simply instructed to weigh them like any other evidence. Despite a total lack of corroborating evidence, the all-white jury had convicted the defendants and sentenced them to death; the Mississippi Supreme Court affirmed the verdicts.

Although the state of Mississippi argued that the U.S. Supreme Court lacked jurisdiction because criminal procedure was under the purview of the states, the justices could hardly ignore the deplorable treatment endured by the *Brown* defendants. Chief Justice Charles Evans Hughes expressed the horror of his colleagues when he observed in his opinion that "the transcript reads more like pages torn from some medieval account than a record made within the confines of a modern civilization." He continued, "It would be difficult to conceive of methods more revolting to the sense of justice than those taken to procure the confessions of these petitioners, and the use of the confessions thus obtained as the basis for conviction and sentence was a clear denial of due process."[2]

But the court did not refer to the voluntariness test in framing the question posed by the case. Its unanimous decision to overturn the convictions of the *Brown* defendants made no mention of the *Wan* case or the Fifth Amendment. Hughes stated the issue as "whether convictions which rest solely upon confessions shown to have been extorted by officers of the State by brutality and violence are consistent with the due process of law required by the Fourteenth Amendment." The upshot was that the standard governing confessions admitted in state courts would henceforth, for all practical purposes, be the same as that of the federal courts.[3]

The Supreme Court continued to hear case after case in which law enforcement ran roughshod over individual rights due to the lack of specificity in that standard. *Brown* had sent a strong signal to the states but in no way had it ended coerced confessions. If anything, the introduction of the due process test, which attempted to assess the fairness of the process through which the confession was obtained, actually muddied the waters even more. Assessing police behavior and its effects on a diverse collection of defendants more or less required a case-by-case analysis. Nor did the due process test supplant the voluntariness principle. In the dozens of cases heard in the three decades following *Brown v. Mississippi* that involved the admissibility of confessions, the court vacillated between assessing voluntariness and fairness.[4]

In *Ashcraft v. Tennessee*, for example, heard in 1944, the court invoked the voluntariness test. The case involved the murder conviction of a man whose confession was elicited through continuous relay interrogations over a thirty-six-hour period. The detectives and prosecutors took time off to sleep but the defendant was denied any rest. Instead of throwing the confession out, however, the judge had put the question of its voluntariness to a jury. The story was eerily reminiscent of Ziang Sung Wan's treatment by the Washington DC police and the trial court. The 1944 Supreme Court found that the circumstances of the man's interrogation were inherently coercive and reversed the verdict, although three justices dissented.[5]

Nearly two decades later, in *Haynes v. Washington* and *Culombe v. Connecticut*, the court looked to the due process standard. In the former, it overruled the State of Washington Supreme Court, which had sustained the verdict against a man found guilty of robbing a gas station. He had been convicted on the strength of a confession wrung from him after police refused his request for an attorney and denied him all contact with the outside world for several days. In the latter case, a thirty-six-year-old "mental defective of the moron class" was held without counsel and questioned intermittently for more than four days, even though he had requested a lawyer; he was later found guilty of murder. As in *Ashcraft*, the voluntariness of the confessions was left to juries to decide, but the court determined that their admission into evidence violated the defendants' due process rights.[6]

The court's frustration and weariness are evident from Justice Felix Frankfurter's opinion in *Culombe*:

> Once again the Court is confronted with the painful duty of sitting in judgment on a State's conviction for murder, after a jury's verdict was found flawless by the State's highest court, in order to determine whether the defendant's confessions, decisive for the

conviction, were admitted into evidence in accordance with the standards for admissibility demanded by the Due Process Clause of the Fourteenth Amendment. This recurring problem touching the administration of criminal justice by the States presents in an aggravated form in this case the anxious task of reconciling the responsibility of the police for ferreting out crime with the right of the criminal defendant, however guilty, to be tried according to constitutional requirements.[7]

It was not until 1964 that the court finally got around to stating *explicitly* that the states were bound to uphold the Fifth Amendment's guarantee against self-incrimination. In *Malloy v. Hogan*, a case that had nothing to do with confessions per se, a Connecticut man, on probation after serving three months in jail for illegal gambling, refused to testify in a state inquiry into criminal activities because doing so might have incriminated him. He was found in contempt of court and sent to prison until he agreed to do so. His petition for a writ of habeas corpus was denied; the rejection was upheld on appeal. In a 5–4 opinion that characterized the American legal system as "accusatorial, not inquisitorial," the court held that states were obliged to honor the Fifth Amendment's protection against self-incrimination in their criminal proceedings.[8]

The muddle created by these disparate approaches and the lack of a bright-line test for police, prosecutors, and judges virtually guaranteed that the lower courts could continue to find ways of admitting the confessions of defendants mistreated between arrest and trial. It became palpably clear that voluntariness required more definition; in order to ensure it, police behavior would again have to be explicitly addressed. But this time the remedy would not involve outlawing nefarious police practices that might *negate* voluntariness so much as mandating constructive behavior that would serve to *ensure* it.[9]

For much of the 1950s and nearly all of the following decade, the Supreme Court was under the leadership of Earl Warren, a Republican progressive who served nearly three terms as governor of California before assuming the position of chief justice. The Warren court, made up largely of New Deal liberals appointed by Democratic pres-

F<small>IG</small>. 32. Chief Justice of the Supreme Court Earl Warren, author of the
Miranda v. Arizona decision. Source: Harvard Law School Library.

idents, was notable for its broad, groundbreaking rulings and its willingness to reexamine and reaffirm the rights of defendants in state and local prosecutions. Warren himself turned out to be far more liberal than anyone had expected when he was appointed. It was a far cry from the Taft court. The Warren court's many landmark decisions expanded civil rights, civil liberties, and federal power in myriad ways.

In 1966, the court granted petitions for writs of certiorari in four more cases of incommunicado interrogation. In each, a defendant in police custody had been cut off from the outside world and questioned without being informed of his rights. Like Ziang Sung Wan, all four defendants had made incriminating statements that were used to convict them. The cases were handpicked and consolidated because they offered an opportunity for the court to spell out procedures for assuring that individuals were accorded their Fifth Amendment rights against self-incrimination. Chief Justice Warren, who wrote the opinion for the majority, asserted that the cases raised questions that "go to the roots of our concepts of American criminal jurisprudence: the restraints society must observe consistent with the Federal Constitution in prosecuting individuals for crime."[10]

The opinions of the Warren court in the four cases were subsumed under one landmark decision, named for the one listed first on the docket: *Miranda v. Arizona*. In the *Miranda* case, a signed confession was used to convict Ernesto Miranda, a man accused of kidnapping and rape who had had no attorney and had not been advised of his right to counsel.

More than four decades after the *Wan* case, and a quarter-century after Brandeis's death, the learned justice's words were central to the court's reasoning. In his opinion, in which he was joined by four other justices, Chief Justice Warren traced the evolution of the privilege against self-incrimination, noting its ancient roots and its search for "the proper scope of governmental power over the citizen." He remarked that the constitutional foundation underlying the privilege "is the respect a government—state or federal—must accord to the dignity and integrity of its citizens."

He traced the principle through the *Bram* case, in which protection against self-incrimination had been found in the Fifth Amendment, and ultimately the *Wan* case, in which it had finally been divorced from specific police misconduct, distilled, and allowed to stand on its own. He quoted the very same excerpt from Brandeis's opinion that the Wickersham Commission had selected so many years earlier:

> In the Federal courts the requisite of voluntariness is not satisfied
> by establishing merely that the confession was not induced by a

promise or a threat. A confession is voluntary in law if, and only if, it was, in fact, voluntarily made. A confession may have been given voluntarily, although it was made to police officers, while in custody, and in answer to an examination conducted by them. But a confession obtained by compulsion must be excluded, whatever may have been the character of the compulsion and whether the compulsion was applied in a judicial proceeding or otherwise.

The chief justice noted that "the current practice of incommunicado interrogation is at odds with one of our Nation's most cherished principles—that the individual may not be compelled to incriminate himself. Unless adequate protective devices are employed to dispel the compulsion inherent in custodial surroundings, no statement obtained from the defendant can truly be the product of his free choice."

He went on to spell out those safeguards, which were ultimately condensed into the summary statement familiar to most Americans today as "Miranda rights." Warren did not make them up out of whole cloth; he reviewed standard procedures of the Federal Bureau of Investigation—the name given the former Bureau of Investigation in 1935—and consulted police training manuals to determine their best practices. They serve to inform suspects in clear and unequivocal terms that they have a right to remain silent, that anything they say might be used against them in a court of law, that they have the right to counsel, and that, if they are unable to afford one, an attorney will be appointed for them.[11]

Ironically, the issue had come full circle from 1884's *Hopt v. Utah*, which had also concerned itself with police conduct. The difference was that *Hopt* was all about what the police should *not* do in order to ensure voluntary confessions; *Miranda* was about what they *had* to do.

The principle articulated so succinctly and elegantly in *Ziang Sung Wan v. United States* was at the heart of the *Miranda* decision, which finally blended the voluntariness and fairness standards. All the new requirements imposed on law enforcement were ordained in the service of ensuring that only a voluntary confession might ever be used against a defendant in a court of law.

Wan's tribulations had cost him years of freedom but in part because of them Americans would henceforth be protected from the kind of abusive treatment he had received at the hands of the Washington police nearly half a century earlier. The continued relevance of his story is demonstrated in the fact that his case has been cited in ninety federal and seventy-seven state cases in the ninety-plus years since it was decided.

Ziang Sung Wan was still living when the Supreme Court issued its opinion in *Miranda v. Arizona.* He never knew of the case, still less his own role in shaping the decision. Had he been entitled to *Miranda's* protections in 1919 and been informed of them, it is highly doubtful he would ever have been convicted for the murder of Ben Sen Wu and his life would certainly have taken a dramatically different turn.

But even in 1966 he would have found *Miranda's* safeguards useful had they been available to him. Wan's tribulations had not ended with his return to the land of his birth. The Chinese Communist Party, which had come to power in 1949, had embarked on a systematic persecution of "rightists" and "counterrevolutionaries" in which forced confessions were encouraged and trials were superfluous.

As it happened, even at age seventy-one Wan would have good reason to envy Ernesto Miranda his new protections.

Epilogue

SO WHO KILLED Theodore Wong and his colleagues?

Not the police, the prosecutors, the Justice Department, nor any of the courts that considered the case against Ziang Sung Wan ever conclusively answered the question of who actually killed the three Chinese diplomats.

Although he was suspected of all three homicides, Wan was tried only for the killing of Ben Sen Wu. The Justice Department declined to prosecute him for the murders of Theodore Wong and Chang Hsi Hsie because it concluded that the Wu murder offered the best chance of securing a conviction. It was the only one of the three to which Wan had ever admitted—even though he later recanted his confession—and in any event, the penalty for first-degree murder would be death no matter how many lives had been taken.

After both the second and third trial resulted in hung juries, however, the Justice Department despaired of proving its case and saw no choice but to drop the charges. Wan was released, though never officially exonerated. The mystery of who killed the three diplomats was never solved. Nor is it possible to do so with certainty a century later.

Wan, of course, offered several conflicting versions of the events of January 29, 1919. During his interrogation, he initially denied all knowledge of the murders, then accused a phantom businessman named C. H. Chen before finally allowing that he himself had murdered Wu, but only, he insisted, after Wu had dispatched his two colleagues. At trial he denied even this and returned to his original narrative: that he had not been at the mission house when the killings took place and had no idea who was responsible. He then stuck to that story throughout his long incarceration, at both of his subsequent trials, and during his later retelling of events in the *Washington Times*, asserting that the confession had been a ruse, offered up merely to put an end to the suffering the police were visiting on his brother and him.

Of all the versions of the story, however, the most credible by far is the one to which he actually confessed soon after the crime was committed. The available evidence points convincingly to a scenario in which Wan and Wu conspired to steal money from the Chinese Educational Mission; in which their plans were foiled; in which Wu used his own revolver to shoot both of his colleagues to death; and in which Wan subsequently murdered Wu with the same gun.

The principal reason for believing that Wan and Wu were working together to embezzle money was that neither probably had the where-withal to pull the scheme off alone. Wan, in residence at the mission house for only a few days and ailing throughout his stay, would not likely have known how the organization handled the disbursement of funds, where the checkbook was kept, how much money was in the account, or which bank handled the mission's business. Wan would have needed Wu to explain the mission's routines.

For his part, Wu was language-challenged—he spoke very little English when he arrived in America. He may have needed Wan to fill out the check and the stub convincingly, to help write the letter that was presented to the bank, and to cash the check, the fateful errand for which Wan's hapless brother was ultimately recruited. In addition, there is reason to believe the relationship between the two men was a close one and that money had changed hands between them in the past.

As far as the murders of Wong and Hsie were concerned, Wu had far more reason to kill the two men than Wan did. If the pair had indeed discovered the missing check, as Wan asserted, Wu would have had every reason to fear the loss of his job and his scholarship and the possibility of being sent back to China in disgrace. After seeing the note left at the mission by Detective Bradley promising to return the next day, he might well also have feared prosecution in America. In addition, Wu was known to have had a rocky relationship at least with Hsie, if not with Wong. It was also his gun that was used to kill the men.

Wan was probably no fan of Dr. Wong but there is no reason to believe that any resentments he may have borne toward the older man would have risen to the level of a motive for murder. He certainly lacked money but he would not have needed to kill for it: there was always his wealthy mother back in Shanghai. And the discovery of the stolen check would not have pointed to him. There was no other obvious reason for him to pull the trigger on Wong, still less Hsie, whom he had known for only a few days.

And as for the murder of Wu, who else could have done it but Wan? Shortly after he accused C. H. Chen, he abandoned that ruse and never returned to it during his trial. No credible alternative theory of the case was presented in any of Wan's three trials. Although doing so was not the responsibility of the defense counsel, Lambert, Wan's attorney, did all he could to leave the jury with the impression that Kang Li might have played a role in the killing. But he fell far short of leveling a credible accusation at him. And Senator Stanley's summation, while effective, amounted to little more than a play for sympathy. Even Wan's own postmortem in the *Washington Times*, which came closest to pointing the finger at Kang Li, was more of an indictment of the methods of the DC Police Department than it was a convincing charge.

If Wan had indeed killed all three men in cold blood, it bought him nothing to confess to only one murder. The penalty—death by hanging and, subsequently, in the electric chair—would have been the same. And then there is the fact of his palpable relief after unburdening himself, his immediate assertion that he was ready to plead guilty and "take his medicine" and his declaration that he did not intend even to hire an attorney. It was only after he realized that the government intended to prosecute his brother for murder as well that he changed his mind about this.

Wan's subsequent recanting of his confession smacks far more of a tactic to secure acquittal than it does of a genuine change of heart. In all likelihood, his statement was an accurate description of how the three men had met their untimely end.

So why celebrate a case in which a murderer got off?

The importance of the case of *Ziang Sung Wan v. United States* does not hinge on the defendant's guilt or innocence. A system that presumes innocence until guilt is proven must of necessity provide protections against false conviction, even at the price of the occasional failure to convict the guilty.

Coercion often leads to false confessions, which pervert the judicial process and can send innocent people to jail or to their deaths. In the 1920s false confessions were thought to be quite rare, but modern science has provided incontrovertible evidence otherwise. With the availability of post-conviction DNA testing, it is now often possible to prove the innocence of the wrongly convicted. The Innocence Project, a national litigation and public policy organization, has found that false confessions played a role in about 25 percent of such cases. The figure for juveniles under eighteen is closer to 40 percent. The lion's share occur in homicide cases.[1]

But reliability is only part of the equation. There is also the question of rights and knowledge of them. Thanks to television, *Miranda* warnings have become enshrined in our national culture; many Americans are well aware that they are under no compulsion to talk with an arresting officer. But not all are. Young, uneducated, and mentally compromised defendants are less likely to be aware of such rights, as are foreigners. *Miranda* mandates that all accused persons be told of them, permitting them to make an informed choice and ensuring that their dignity is protected.

Miranda, in no way perfect, goes a long way toward ensuring voluntariness, which the *Wan* case established clearly was the proper criterion for inclusion of a confession in a trial. Thanks in part to *Wan*, safeguards are now in place to prevent the abuse of the accused and the myriad, nefarious ways that confessions can pried from them.

So did Ziang Sung Wan get away with murder?

Assuming Wan did kill at least Ben Sen Wu, if not the other two men, it is true that he escaped the electric chair, which would have been his fate under the laws of the District of Columbia had either the second or third jury found him guilty of murder in the first degree. But he did serve seven years in DC jail with the threat of execution hanging over his head, sometimes only a day away. And that, as it turned out, was only the beginning of his trials. Wan's later life was no bed of roses. Had he known what fate lay in store for him when he returned to China permanently in 1929, he might well have made a different choice.

Back in Shanghai, Wan married and fathered three daughters, but during the Japanese occupation of the 1930s his family lost their home and land. Rampant inflation forced them to sell off many personal belongings; on several occasions they did not have enough to eat. After the war, Wan secured a job at the foreign relations office of the Shanghai municipal government. In 1946, he applied for a job at the American consulate but there were no openings. When the Nationalist government withdrew to Taiwan and the People's Republic of China was established in 1949, he naturally lost his position with the local government. After a period of unemployment, he found work with a tea-exporting company and, in 1951, his savings almost completely depleted, a medical supply factory.

His last letter to his former attorney Charles Fahy was written in September that year. There would be no more correspondence, because shortly afterward he fell victim to the Campaign to Suppress Counterrevolutionaries, the first political movement launched by the newly ascendant Chinese Communist Party to eradicate enemies real and perceived. He was detained and sent without trial to a "reform through labor" camp in Jiangsu Province. Having worked for the hated Nationalists and lived abroad, he was an obvious target. He remained in the camp, where "class enemies" and "counterrevolutionaries" accused of trying to undermine the government were incarcerated, from the early 1950s until 1964. Then, nearing seventy years of age, he took ill, was granted medical parole, and was sent back to Shanghai—not to be freed but to be imprisoned there. He died in June 1968, soon after the onset of the Great Proletarian Cultural Revolution—a violent political movement that plunged China into chaos for a decade—poor, ill, and miserable.

Others who played roles in Wan's ordeals fared somewhat better in subsequent years. Some were already near the end of their careers when their paths crossed with Wan's; others went on to greater achievements:

Louis D. Brandeis's opinion in *Ziang Sung Wan v. United States* was written eight years into his twenty-three-year career as associate justice of the Supreme Court. He would serve until 1939, drafting an additional 295 opinions before he retired. Brandeis, who lived to see many of his progressive ideas incorporated into law, died of a heart attack two years after he retired from the bench. His remains, together with those of his wife, are interred beneath the portico of the University of Louisville School of Law, which bears his name and also houses his collected papers.

Guy E. Burlingame, one of Wan's police interrogators, was suspended from the force in 1929 after being charged with mistreating a woman with whom he was having a love affair. Burlingame, who was married, was accused of scheming to steal from her and threatening to kill her. The accusations led to broader allegations of corruption in the DC police force; the matter was investigated by a special police trial board and a grand jury. Ultimately, both bodies dismissed the charges and Burlingame retired later that year. He died at the age of seventy-six and is buried in Franklinville, New York.[2]

Zechariah Chafee Jr. went on, after his assignment with the Wickersham Commission, to draft the Federal Interpleader Act of 1936, designed to resolve multiple claims against insurance companies, banks, and other corporations. He was a member of the United Nations Sub-Commission on Freedom of Information and the Press and a delegate to the United Nations Conference on Freedom of Information in 1948. In 1952, Senator Joseph McCarthy (R-WI) called him "dangerous to America." He died in 1957 at the age of seventy-two in his home in Cambridge, Massachusetts.[3]

After **John W. Davis** lost the 1924 presidential election to incumbent Calvin Coolidge in a landslide, he returned to private practice and represented many large U.S. corporations. He adopted Cyrus R. Vance, the son of his late cousin, who later became secretary of state under President Jimmy Carter. Davis argued 140 cases before the Supreme Court in the course of his legal career and is best remembered for his final appearance in the case of *Brown v. Board of Education*, in which he fruitlessly defended the "separate but equal" doctrine. He died at the age of eighty-one in 1955 and is interred in Locust Valley, New York.

William Cullen Dennis, a member of the legal team that appealed Wan's case to the Supreme Court, became president of Earlham College in 1929 and served until 1946. A Republican and a Quaker, he was an authority on international law. In later life he received honorary degrees from Earlam, Depauw, Indiana, and Butler universities and Wabash College. He is buried in Richmond, Indiana.

Charles Fahy, on Wan's legal team from beginning to end, tried his hand at a book chronicling the case. With Wan's full support he wrote seven chapters but never finished the manuscript. Fahy left Washington shortly after the charges against Wan were dropped, returning in 1933 to accept an appointment as assistant solicitor for the Department of the Interior. He later served as general counsel of the National Labor Relations Board and in 1941 was appointed the twenty-sixth solicitor general of the United States by President Franklin D. Roosevelt. He served until 1945, when he was asked to direct the legal division of the U.S. Group Control Council in Germany in the aftermath of World War II. In 1949, he was appointed to the U.S. Court of Appeals for the DC Circuit by President Harry Truman. He died in 1979 and is buried in Arlington National Cemetery.[4]

Peyton Gordon, who appeared before the U.S. Supreme Court for the government in the *Wan* case, was nominated by President Calvin Coolidge in 1928 to the seat on the United States District Court for the District of Columbia vacated by Adolph A. Hoehling, the judge who had freed Wan. He served on the court for thirteen years. He died at seventy-six in 1946 and is buried in Arlington National Cemetery.[5]

Detective **Clifford L. Grant** lived long enough to see the U.S. Supreme Court throw out the confession he and his colleagues had labored so hard to extract from Ziang Sung Wan but not long enough to testify at either of Wan's subsequent trials. He was stricken with a heart attack at his office and died the next day. His funeral at the Scottish Rite Cathedral was so well attended that 200 people were forced to stand outside. He is buried in Rock Creek Cemetery, Washington DC.[6]

Most of Judge **Adolph A. Hoehling Jr.**'s career was behind him when he set Ziang Sung Wan free in 1926. He resigned from the United States District Court for the District of Columbia the following year and returned to private practice. He lived until 1941 and, due to his service in World War I, is buried in Arlington National Cemetery.

George D. Horning Jr., who assisted Major Peyton Gordon in prosecuting Wan's second and third trials, resigned from the U.S. Attorney's office in 1927 and joined Wan's defense attorney Wilton J. Lambert's law firm. He also became a professor of law at American University. In 1973, during the Watergate investigation, United States District Court for the District of Columbia Chief Justice John J. Sirica asked Horning, a former colleague, to represent him in a dispute with the White House over the release of President Richard Nixon's tapes. He died the following year and is interred in Arlington National Cemetery.[7]

Edward J. Kelly, one of the detectives who investigated the *Wan* case, had reason to be grateful to James A. O'Shea, Wan's attorney, for O'Shea's defense of him in a 1929 grand jury investigation into an accusation of bungling a murder investigation. Kelly went on to be appointed chief of police in 1941. He died of a heart attack less than three weeks after retiring from a forty-year career with the department. He is buried in Glenwood Cemetery, Washington DC.[8]

Wilton J. Lambert, whom the *New York Times* called an "intimate of presidents," lived for nearly another decade after defending Wan in his two final trials. A multitalented attorney, he was as comfortable defending corporations as he was accused criminals. Lambert represented William Randolph Hearst's interests in Washington as well as those of the *New York Sun* and the *New York Times* and served as a director of the Washington Post Corporation. He died at home at sixty-three and is buried in Rock Creek Cemetery, Washington DC.[9]

John E. Laskey served as U. S. attorney until 1921, when he went into private practice with his son. He received an honorary degree from Georgetown University the year before his death; he had taught at the university's law school since 1910. He is interred in Brentwood, Maryland.[10]

Bolitha J. Laws, the assistant U.S. attorney who helped prosecute the 1919 murder trial, had an illustrious career in and out of government. He left the Justice Department in 1920 and spent most of the next two decades in private practice but was nominated by President Franklin D. Roosevelt to a new seat on the United States District Court for the District of Columbia, a position he assumed in 1938. Roosevelt later elevated him to chief justice in 1945. The court was reorganized in 1948 but he continued to serve it as a judge until his death in 1958.

Dr. Kang Li had returned to Tsinghua University, his alma mater, and was working as a physician there when he was summoned to the United States to testify as star witness for the prosecution in Ziang Sung Wan's second and third trials. Dr. Li enacted revolutionary changes at Tsinghua's medical clinic and married the daughter of the university president. He later became an assistant professor at Nanking Central University (today's Nanjing University) and an officer of the Shanghai YMCA Hospital, eventually going into private practice. He is said to have committed suicide some time in the late 1930s or early 1940s, during the Japanese occupation of Shanghai.[11]

Frederic D. McKenney, who participated in oral arguments in Wan's Supreme Court case, continued to argue cases before the court and served several of its justices as a personal attorney. He was special counsel for the Pennsylvania Railroad and a director of Riggs National Bank. McKenney died after a long illness at the age of eighty-six at his home in Washington's Kennedy-Warren Apartments, about a mile north of the building on Kalorama Road that had housed the Chinese Educational Mission. He is buried in Oak Hill Cemetery, Washington DC.[12]

Rev. Peter J. O'Callaghan eventually left his position at Catholic University but continued his lifelong anti-alcohol crusade from his retirement home in Oakland, New Jersey. He traveled to Torrington, Connecticut, in 1931 to attend the sixtieth annual convention of the Catholic Total Abstinence Union of America and died there of acute indigestion.[13]

Wan was not the only young man who owed a debt to **Hugh A. O'Donnell**, a "one-man employment agency" who used his wide circle of friends to help find jobs for hundreds of Notre Dame graduates like himself and other young men. O'Donnell suffered a stroke at the age of sixty-seven and died less than a week later. Three hundred people, including many New York luminaries, attended his requiem mass at the Church of the Blessed Sacrament on West 71st Street in Manhattan; he was buried in Brooklyn's Greenwood Cemetery.[14]

James A. O'Shea survived his summary firing by Ziang Sung Wan after his successful appeal to the Supreme Court and remained a familiar figure around the DC courts for another quarter-century. Known as "Mr. Courthouse," O'Shea defended hundreds of people accused of murder during his four-decade-long career. When he died in Washington at the age of seventy-one, attorney Charles Fahy was one of his pallbearers.[15]

Raymond W. Pullman, chief of the Washington DC police force and lead interrogator of Ziang Sung Wan, contracted double pneumonia after a bout of influenza and died of a blood clot in his heart less than two months after Wan's conviction. He was only thirty-seven years old. U.S. Attorney John E. Laskey eulogized him as "an energetic, progressive, clean public official." He is buried in Congressional Cemetery, Washington DC.[16]

Most of the professional life of **A. Owsley Stanley**, the former senator, former congressman, and former governor of Kentucky who brought jurors to tears during Wan's final trial, was behind him by 1926. He returned to legal practice after his unsuccessful bid for reelection to the Senate in 1924; subsequent attempts at reelection to the Senate were also failures. In 1930, he was appointed by President Herbert Hoover to the International Joint Commission, which adjudicated boundary disputes between the United States and Canada; he eventually chaired the organization, which he served until 1954. He died in 1958 and is buried in Frankfort, Kentucky.

Because of his brother's troubles, **Tsong Ing Van** decided to go by the Americanized name of Thomas I. Van. After the charges against the two were dropped, he went briefly, like his brother, into the confectionery business in Washington. When that venture folded, he returned to New York and opened a catering business, which also failed; by 1931 he was back in Washington. The following year he married an American divorcée but separated from her after a few weeks.

The legality of the marriage was questioned when a cabaret singer with whom he had once cohabited came forward with a claim that she was his common-law wife. In 1936, before a planned visit to China, he applied for a right-to-return certificate based on his marriage. But because the couple had not lived together continuously after they wed, his application was denied, which meant that if he left the country he would not be permitted to return. He does not appear to have made the trip. In 1950, while working as secretary to the proprietor of a Chinese employment agency, Van became a founder of the Chinese League of America, a not-for-profit membership association incorporated in New York to "foster the fundamentals and ideals of American citizenship and the Constitution of the United States" among America's Chinese and thus prepare them for naturalization. What became of him after that is unclear.[17]

Seven months after he decided the *Wan* case, Court of Appeals judge **Josiah Van Orsdel** rendered the decision for which he is best known. In the case of *Frye v. United States*, in which a trial court judge had disallowed testimony based on a lie-detector examination, Van Orsdel established what became known as the "Frye standard," a test to determine the admissibility of novel scientific evidence. The following year, he became president of the District of Columbia Sons of the American Revolution and subsequently served as president general of the national organization. He remained on the bench until his death in 1937.

The *Miranda* decision was issued late in the sixteen-year Supreme Court career of Chief Justice **Earl Warren**, who stepped down from the court three years later. He lived for only five more years. He died in 1974 and is interred at Arlington National Cemetery.

George W. Wickersham was close to the end of his career and his life when he chaired the commission that bore his name. He went on to head the Council on Foreign Relations and the New York State Economic Council. He was also one of the guardians of the property of the heiress Gloria Vanderbilt, then eleven years old, and an unwilling party in the suit for custody of the child filed by her mother. He died of a heart attack in a Manhattan taxi at the age of seventy-seven and is buried in Englewood, New Jersey.[18]

CHRONOLOGY

1916

APRIL 8

Theodore T. Wong, Ben Sen Wu, and Ziang Sung Wan arrive in North America. Wong and Wu proceed to Washington DC and join Chang Hsi Hsie at the Chinese Educational Mission. Wan joins his brother, Tsong Ing Van, in Ohio.

1917

Wan earns a bachelor's degree from Ohio Northern University and moves to New York City.

1918

Van withdraws from Ohio Wesleyan University and joins Wan in New York. The brothers invest in a theater in Brooklyn, which soon fails. Wan contracts the Spanish flu.

1919

JANUARY 22

Wan visits Washington DC as a guest of Ben Sen Wu and stays at the Chinese Educational Mission for five days.

JANUARY 27

Wan leaves the mission and checks into the Harris Hotel, near Union Station.

JANUARY 29

Van joins Wan in Washington after being summoned. Kang Li, a classmate of Hsie and Wu, calls at the mission. Wan answers the door and tells him no one is home.

Wu has dinner with friends at the Oriental Restaurant and returns to the mission at about 8:00 p.m. Wong and Hsie dine at the Nankin Restaurant, departing a few minutes after 10:00 p.m.

Wong, Hsie, and Wu are shot to death at the Chinese Educational Mission.

JANUARY 30

Van presents a check for $5,000 to Riggs National Bank, drawn on the account of the Chinese Educational Mission. The bank, suspecting forgery, refuses to cash it.

Wan and Van return to New York by train.

JANUARY 31

Wong is found dead at the mission by Kang Li. Police discover that Hsie and Wu have also been killed. Wan is an immediate suspect. DC police detectives Edward Kelly and Guy Burlingame depart for New York in search of him.

FEBRUARY 1

Wan is found in New York, sick in bed. He returns voluntarily to Washington at the urging of Kelly and Burlingame. He is questioned on arrival by Chief of Police Major Raymond W. Pullman and Inspector Clifford L. Grant in the presence of Kelly and Burlingame.

Police gather forensic evidence from the murder scene. Coroner conducts autopsies on victims.

FEBRUARY 2

Wan is detained under guard at the Dewey Hotel by Washington police and questioned incessantly, despite his illness.

FEBRUARY 3

Van is brought from New York and also detained at the Dewey Hotel. The two are not permitted to meet.

FEBRUARY 8

Wan and Van are taken to the murder scene and questioned aggressively. The two are treated badly by the detectives and Wan is not permitted to sleep.

FEBRUARY 9

Under duress, Wan confesses to forgery and admits to having been present during the murders, but does not reveal the name of the killer.

Wan and Van are arrested.

FEBRUARY 10

Wan confesses only to the murder of Ben Sen Wu, whom he blames for the other deaths, and attempts to exonerate his brother.

FEBRUARY 11

Coroner's jury holds Wan and Van for action by the grand jury in the triple murder. Defendants are taken to DC Jail.

SEPTEMBER 30

Wan is indicted by the grand jury for the three murders.

OCTOBER 7

Represented by attorneys James A. O'Shea and Charles Fahy, Wan is arraigned for the murder of Ben Sen Wu in the Supreme Court of the District of Columbia, pleading not guilty. Van is arraigned on a charge of forgery, and is placed under $3,000 bond.

OCTOBER 10

Van is released on bail and returns to New York.

DECEMBER 9

The trial of Wan for the murder of Ben Sen Wu begins in DC Supreme Court.

DECEMBER 16

A jury is empaneled and testimony begins.

1920

JANUARY 9

Jury finds Wan guilty of murder after deliberating for only a half hour.

JANUARY 10

U.S. District Attorney John E. Laskey announces that Van will be tried for forgery.

JANUARY 14

Attorneys for Wan file for a new trial on several grounds, including the assertion that Wan's confession should not have been admitted into evidence because it had been forced.

MAY 7

Judge Ashley M. Gould denies the motion for a new trial.

MAY 14

Wan is sentenced to be hanged on December 1, 1920.

NOVEMBER 27

Wan's execution is stayed, pending an appeal.

1921

MAY 20

Judge Gould dies without having acted on the Bill of Exceptions, necessary for an appeal.

NOVEMBER 16

A delegation including members of the Anthony League and religious leaders seeks President Warren G. Harding's intercession in the cases of four men in DC jail facing execution, including Wan, because of the "barbarity of capital punishment." Harding refuses to consider the plea.

NOVEMBER 22

Counsel for Wan moves to vacate the previous judgment, set aside the verdict, and grant a new trial, because of the death of the trial judge before the Bill of Exceptions was settled.

NOVEMBER 30

Chief Justice Walter J. McCoy of the DC Supreme Court signs Bill of Exceptions.

1922

APRIL 3

Appeal is made to the Court of Appeals of the District of Columbia.

1923

MAY 1

The forgery case against Van is called before the DC Supreme

Court, but put on hold at the request of the U.S. attorney, pending the result of Wan's appeal.

MAY 7

DC Court of Appeals affirms Wan's conviction and death sentence.

MAY 26

Court of Appeals denies a Writ of Error.

JULY 23

Defendant's legal team, now including John W. Davis, seeks review of the *Wan* case by the U.S. Supreme Court.

OCTOBER 15

U.S. Supreme Court agrees to review the case.

1924

APRIL 7, 8

Ziang Sung Wan v. United States, 266 U.S. 1 (1924), is argued before the U.S. Supreme Court.

OCTOBER 13

U.S. Supreme Court overturns lower court decision and orders a new trial for Wan. Unanimous opinion is written by Justice Louis D. Brandeis.

1925

JANUARY 30

President Calvin Coolidge signs legislation substituting the electric chair for hanging as punishment for capital offenses in the District of Columbia.

OCTOBER

Kang Li returns to the United States from China to appear in a new trial.

1926

JANUARY 11

Retrial of Wan begins in DC Supreme Court.

FEBRUARY 11

Jury is unable to reach a unanimous verdict and is discharged. Majority favors acquittal.

APRIL 12

Wan is tried for a third time in DC Supreme Court for the murder of Ben Sen Wu.

MAY 13

Hung jury, 9–3 in favor of acquittal, is discharged.

MAY 27

Defense counsel Lambert moves to dismiss the charges against Wan.

JUNE 16

U.S. Attorney's office drops all charges against Wan and Van. DC Supreme Court orders Wan's immediate release after more than seven years in prison.

DECEMBER

Wan goes into the confectionery business.

1927

MAY 26

Ziang Sung Wan, Inc. is incorporated in the state of Delaware.

1928

Wan departs for China.

1929

MARCH 15

Wan arrives in the United States to wind down his affairs. He soon returns to China permanently.

1931

JUNE 25

The National Commission on Law Observance and Enforcement, a.k.a. the Wickersham Commission, issues its report, *Lawlessness in Law Enforcement*, which includes an extensive discussion of *Ziang Sung Wan v. United States*.

1932

NOVEMBER 7

The Supreme Court decides the case of *Powell v. Alabama*, and for the first time reverses a state criminal conviction for a violation of a criminal procedural provision of the Bill of Rights.

1936

FEBRUARY 17

The Supreme Court rules in the case of *Brown v. Mississippi* that an involuntary confession extracted by police violence violates the Fourteenth Amendment and may not be admitted into evidence in state and local courts.

1966

JUNE 13

Supreme Court issues decision in the case of *Miranda v. Arizona*, setting out procedures to be followed by law enforcement to protect defendants from self-incrimination and to render any custodial confessions admissible in court.

1968

JUNE

Ziang Sung Wan dies in Shanghai.

ACKNOWLEDGMENTS

FIRST AND FOREMOST, I would like to acknowledge my debt to two brilliant young attorneys who were invaluable in helping this non-lawyer understand not only the ins and outs and implications of the case of *Ziang Sung Wan v. United States*, but where it fit into the progression of Supreme Court cases governing criminal confessions and the relationships of these cases to one another.

The first, Joshua N. Friedman, worked side by side with me and shared my excitement as we pored over century-old documents relating to the *Wan* case in the National Archives and the Library of Congress—some in Justice Brandeis's own handwriting. He explained the procedures of the trial court, the appellate court, and the Supreme Court, and it was he who months into the research—first noted the direct link between the case and the *Miranda* decision. The second, Eli Blood-Patterson, conducted research on all of the court's rulings with regard to the admissibility of confessions over the better part of a century, and walked me expertly through the evolution of this important but confusing area of law.

Nor were these the only attorneys I consulted in the course of thinking about and writing the book. I am exceedingly grateful to the other members of my legal "dream team," which Ziang Sung Wan himself might have envied: Diane Ambler, Ira Belkin, Marsha Cohan, Russell DaSilva, Claudia Gilman, Richard Gordin, Steven Herman, Paul Seligman, Deborah Strauss, Eugene Theroux, and Alice Thurston.

Much appreciation goes to Professor York Lo for his research on the family of Dr. Theodore Ting Wong and for his kind introduction to several of Dr. Wong's descendants, among them Wilfred Ling, Daniel Kwok, Erica Ling, and Wade Loo, all of whom were more than happy to share what information and materials they had inherited. I am also indebted to Stephen Mink, Erica's husband, for offering up his own research into the life and death of Dr. Wong, and for his critical review of the manuscript.

From China, I received immeasurable help in determining the fate of Ziang Sung Wan after his return to China from Eddie Wu (Wu Zhonggao). Vivian Huang (Huang Wei) of the Historical Documents Division of the Shanghai Library was also helpful in this regard, as were Janet Shanberge, Bob Burke, Tess Johnston, Patrick Cranley, and Justin O'Jack, all in Shanghai, and Roy Delbyck, in Hong Kong.

Thanks to the staff of the National Archives, especially Marian Smith and Robert Ellis in Washington, David Langbart and Christina Violeta Jones in College Park, Gloria Legaspi in San Bruno, and Heather Glasby in Philadelphia. Also to Matthew Hofstedt of the Supreme Court, Gary Johnson of the Library of Congress, Mark Greek of the Washington DC Public Library, and William Branch of the Washington DC Office of Public Records.

Many others generously helped locate materials and answered queries, including Emily Gattozzi of Ohio Wesleyan University, Jocelyn K. Wilk of Columbia University, Tiffany Cole of the University of Virginia, Michelle Drobik of Ohio State University, Lynn Conway of Georgetown University, Paul Lodgson of Ohio Northern University, Nancy F. Lyon and Jessica Becker of Yale University, Carol A. Leadenham of Stanford University, and Wang Yajie of Tsinghua University. Also Peter Lee, Allison Gotfried, Vinicius Beraldo, Sharon Holdren, and Gordon Whittaker.

Gratitude is due also to Peter Bernstein, my indefatigable literary agent; to Tom Swanson, Natalie O'Neal, Ann Baker, Rosemary Sekora, Elizabeth Zaleski, and Rachel Gould of Potomac Books and the University of Nebraska Press; and to Vicki Low, my favorite copy editor on the planet.

Finally, special thanks to Nicholas Chen, John Holden, Jane Leung Larson, Lester F. Lau, Peter Lee, Tim Liang, Natalie Lichtenstein, the late Dr. Raymond D. Lum, Cathy Mack, Stephen Markscheid, Edward Rhoads, and Roger W. Sullivan for help and unflagging encouragement throughout the course of the project.

NOTES

The following abbreviations have been employed below for the names of newspapers cited most often.

BDE   *Brooklyn Daily Eagle*
ES   *Evening Star*
NYT   *New York Times*
WDN   *Washington Daily News*
WH   *Washington Herald*
WP   *Washington Post*
WT   *Washington Times*

Preface

1. Oral history interview with Anthony Lewis, conducted by Victor Geminiani, March 18, 1993, National Equal Justice Library, Special Collections, Georgetown University Law Library.

2. "Wan Tells How He Shot Wu After Wu Had Killed Hsie and Doctor Wong," WT, February 10, 1919.

Prologue

1. Nankin Café Display Advertisement, WT, July 2, 1919.

2. "Chinaman's Check a Forgery," WT, February 2, 1919.

1. Three Men in a Tub

1. "Vancouver Celebrates Arrival of Steamship," *San Francisco Call*, June 11, 1913; "Empress of Russia Due on Coast Soon," *Seattle Daily Times*, May 23, 1913; "New Ships Coming," *Oregonian*, February 23, 1913.

2. Ziang Sung Wan, "Wan: His Own Story," WT, July 20, 1926; Edward J. M. Rhoads, *Stepping Forth into the World* (Hong Kong: Hong Kong University Press, 2011), 53 and 96; Chinese Educational Mission Connections website, accessed February 11, 2016, http://www.cemconnections.org/index.php?option=com_content

&task=view&id=160&Itemid=54; Baike.com website, accessed August 11, 2015: http://www.baike.com/wiki/%e5%ae%a6%e7%bb%b4%e5%9f%8e.

3. Three sources have been immensely valuable in charting the early life of Theodore T. Wong; two are unpublished memoirs provided by Wilfred Ling, a grandson of Dr. Wong. These are his own *Dr. and Mrs. Theodore T. T. Wong—A Biographical Sketch*, written in 2005 and revised in 2009; and Ethel Wong Loo, *Memoir of Tante Ethel (Unfinished)*, which he transcribed and edited in 1997. The third is York Lo (羅元旭), *Dong Cheng Xi Jiu: Qige Huaren Jidujiao Jiazu Yu Zhongxi Jiaoliu Bainian* (東成西就—七個華人基督教家族與中西交流百年) (Hong Kong: Joint Publishing, 2012), 39–41.

2. An Unwelcome Guest

1. *Report of the Commissioner of Education for the Year Ended June 30, 1915* (Washington: Government Printing Office, 1915), vol. 1, 747–48; "From the Viewpoint of Association Men," *Association Men* 44 (September 1918): 613.

2. Carroll B. Malone, "The First Remission of the Boxer Indemnity," *The American Historical Review* 32, no. 1 (October 1926): 64–68.

3. Xiaojuan Zhou, *The Influences of the American Boxer Indemnity Reparations on Chinese Higher Education* (master's thesis, University of Nebraska, 2014), 34–35.

4. Xiaojian Zhao and Edward J. W. Park, eds., *Asian Americans: An Encyclopedia of Social, Cultural, Economic and Political History* (Santa Barbara CA: Greenwood Publishing Group, 2013), 523–24.

5. "The Late Director T. T. Wong, Mr. C. H. Hsie and Mr. B. S. Wu of the Chinese Educational Mission," *The Chinese Students' Monthly* 14, no. 5 (March 1919): 287–90.

6. "The Late Director T. T. Wong, Mr. C. H. Hsie and Mr. B. S. Wu of the Chinese Educational Mission," *The Chinese Students' Monthly* 14, no. 5 (March 1919): 287–89.

7. "Methodist," *WT*, March 15, 1913; "Koos Entertain Wong," *ES*, October 19, 1916; "Check Stub to Clear Mystery," *WT*, February 4, 1924.

8. World War I draft registration cards for Ziang Sung Wan, June 5, 1917, and Tsong Ing Van, August 24, 1918, United States World War I Draft Registration Cards, 1917–1918. NARA microfilm publication M1509, National Archives and Records Administration, Washington DC.

9. "Former Salem School Chieftain Testifies for Chinese Student Charged With Triple Murder," [East Liverpool OH] *Evening Review*, May 4, 1926; "Case of the Evil Cats' Eye," *Oregonian*, October 19, 1947.

10. United States v. Ziang Sung Wan, Testimony of Charles Diehl and Israel Weinberg, Supreme Court of the District of Columbia, September 30, 1919.

11. Recollections of Grace Wong Kwok, in a February 25, 2015 email to the author from her son, Daniel Kwok.

12. United States v. Ziang Sung Wan, Testimony of Gertrude Bartels, Supreme Court of the District of Columbia, September 30, 1919.

13. "Police Have Clue in Triple Chinese Murder Mystery," *ES*, February 3, 1919.

14. United States v. Ziang Sung Wan, Testimony of Robert William Miles, Supreme Court of the District of Columbia, September 30, 1919.

15. United States v. Ziang Sung Wan, Testimony of Kang Li, Supreme Court of the District of Columbia, September 30, 1919.

16. United States v. Ziang Sung Wan, Testimony of Bennett G. Dent, George O. Vass and Robert G. Fleming, Supreme Court of the District of Columbia, September 30, 1919.

3. Murder at the Mission

1. Descriptions of the crime scene come from the United States v. Ziang Sung Wan, Testimony of Kang Li, Harry Evans, Fred Sandberg, and Warren O. Embry, Supreme Court of the District of Columbia, September 30, 1919, and Guy E. Burlingame, "The Three Murders that Shocked Washington," *Master Detective*, April 1931.

2. "Wan Tells How He Shot Wu After Wu Had Killed Hsie and Doctor Wong," *wt*, February 10, 1919.

3. Guy E. Burlingame, "The Three Murders that Shocked Washington" *Master Detective*, April 1931.

4. "Notorious Thief Is Found By Detective," *Wichita Eagle*, February 14, 1909.

5. Various accounts of the interview in Wan's room in New York are found in United States v. Ziang Sung Wan, Testimony of Guy E. Burlingame, Edward J. Kelly, Kang Li, Tsong Ing Van, and Ziang Sung Wan, Supreme Court of the District of Columbia, September 30, 1919, and in Guy E. Burlingame, "The Three Murders that Shocked Washington," *Master Detective*, April 1931.

6. "Hired Assassin Killed Chinese Police Theory," *wh*, February 2, 1919; Guy E. Burlingame, "The Three Murders that Shocked Washington," *Master Detective*, April 1931; United States v. Ziang Sung Wan, Testimony of Charles H. Bradley, Supreme Court of the District of Columbia, September 30, 1919.

7. Guy E. Burlingame, "The Three Murders that Shocked Washington," *Master Detective*, April 1931.

8. United States v. Ziang Sung Wan, Testimony of Clifford L. Grant, Supreme Court of the District of Columbia, September 30, 1919.

9. "Chinaman Wan Found in New York," *wt*, February 1, 1919.

4. Incommunicado

1. United States v. Ziang Sung Wan, Testimony of Clifford L. Grant, Supreme Court of the District of Columbia, September 30, 1919; "Hired Assassin Killed Chinese Police Theory," *wh*, February 2, 1919; "Z. S. Wan Stoutly Denies Knowledge of Triple Murder," *es*, February 2, 1919; "Chinaman's Check a Forgery," *wt*, February 2, 1919.

2. "Wan Questioned for Hours on Crime," *wt*, February 2, 1919; "Clear Student of Murder Suspicion," *New York Sun*, February 3, 1919.

3. "Hired Assassin Killed Chinese Police Theory," *wh*, February 2, 1919.

4. "Hired Assassin Killed Chinese Police Theory," *wh*, February 2, 1919.

5. United States v. Ziang Sung Wan, Testimony of Tsong Ing Van, Supreme Court of the District of Columbia, September 30, 1919.

6. "Police Have Clue in Triple Chinese Murder Mystery," ES, February 3, 1919; "Check Stub to Clear Mystery," WT, February 4, 1919.

7. United States v. Ziang Sung Wan, Testimony of Edward J. Kelly, Supreme Court of the District of Columbia, September 30, 1919.

8. "Check Stub to Clear Mystery," WT, February 4, 1919; "Chinese Slayers in Police Grasp," WT, February 5, 1919.

9. "Wan Questioned for Hours on Crime," WT, February 2, 1919; "Arrests of Chinese Slayers Seem Near," WP, February 4, 1919.

10. "Wan Held by Police for Questioning in Murder Case," WH, February 4, 1919.

11. "Check Stub to Clear Mystery," WT, February 4, 1919.

12. "Arrests of Chinese Slayers Seem Near," WP, February 4, 1919; Guy E. Burlingame, "The Three Murders that Shocked Washington," *Master Detective*, May 1931.

13. "Social Service Police Desired," WT, December 21, 1915; "Chinaman's Check a Forgery," WT, February 3, 1919.

5. Interrogation

1. "Laskey Says Evidence in Chinese Case Is Complete," WT, February 9, 1919.

2. "Arrests Are Delayed as New Clue Is Investigated," WT, February 7, 1919; "Laskey Says Evidence in Chinese Case Is Complete," WT, February 9, 1919.

3. "Register in Hotel Murder Evidence," ES, February 5, 1919.

4. United States v. Ziang Sung Wan, Testimony of Raymond W. Pullman, Supreme Court of the District of Columbia, September 30, 1919.

5. United States v. Ziang Sung Wan, Testimony of Edward J. Kelly, Supreme Court of the District of Columbia, September 30, 1919.

6. United States v. Ziang Sung Wan, Testimony of Tsong Ing Van and Ziang Sung Wan, Supreme Court of the District of Columbia, September 30, 1919.

7. "Chinaman's Check a Forgery," WT, February 3, 1919; "Register in Hotel Murder Evidence," ES, February 5, 1919.

8. David Cole, "Are Foreign Nationals Entitled to the Same Constitutional Rights as Citizens?" *Thomas Jefferson Law Review* 25 (2003), 367–88.

9. United States v. Ziang Sung Wan, Testimony of Guy E. Burlingame, Supreme Court of the District of Columbia, September 30, 1919.

10. "Hired Assassin Killed Chinese Police Theory," WH, February 2, 1919; Guy E. Burlingame, "The Three Murders that Shocked Washington," *Master Detective*, May 1931.

11. "Hired Assassin Killed Chinese Police Theory," WH, February 2, 1919; Guy E. Burlingame, "The Three Murders that Shocked Washington," *Master Detective*, May 1931.

12. United States v. Ziang Sung Wan, Testimony of Edward J. Kelly, Guy E. Burlingame and Clifford L. Grant, Supreme Court of the District of Columbia, September 30, 1919.

13. Ziang Sung Wan, "Wan: His Own Story," WT, July 28, 1926.

14. Guy E. Burlingame, "The Three Murders that Shocked Washington," *Master*

Detective, May 1931; United States v. Ziang Sung Wan, Testimony of Edward J. Kelly, Supreme Court of the District of Columbia, September 30, 1919.

15. United States v. Ziang Sung Wan, Testimony of Edward J. Kelly, Raymond W. Pullman, and Clifford L. Grant, Supreme Court of the District of Columbia, September 30, 1919.

16. United States v. Ziang Sung Wan, Testimony of Tsong Ing Van, Supreme Court of the District of Columbia, September 30, 1919.

17. United States v. Ziang Sung Wan, Testimony of Guy E. Burlingame, Supreme Court of the District of Columbia, September 30, 1919.

18. Ziang Sung Wan, "Wan: His Own Story," *WT*, July 28, 1926.

6. Confession

1. "Houdini's Escape from the 10th Precinct," Park View DC website, accessed February 2, 2016, http://parkviewdc.com/2010/10/01/houdinis-escape-from-the-10th -precinct.

2. United States v. Ziang Sung Wan, Testimony of Clifford L. Grant, Supreme Court of the District of Columbia, September 30, 1919.

3. United States v. Ziang Sung Wan, Testimony of Clifford L. Grant, Supreme Court of the District of Columbia, September 30, 1919.

4. "Held in Triple Murder," *Baltimore Sun*, February 10, 1919.

5. "Wan Tells How He Shot Wu After Wu Had Killed Hsie and Doctor Wong," *WT*, February 10, 1919; United States v. Ziang Sung Wan, Testimony of Guy E. Burlingame and Statement of Z. S. Wan Made to Detective Sergeants Guy E. Burlingame and E. J. Kelly in Witness-Room of Tenth Precinct Station on February 11, 1919, Supreme Court of the District of Columbia, September 30, 1919.

6. "Wan Tells How He Shot Wu After Wu Had Killed Hsie and Doctor Wong," *WT*, February 10, 1919.

7. "Insists Van Had Nothing to Do With the Killing," *WT*, February 12, 1919.

8. Ziang Sung Wan, "Wan: His Own Story," *WT*, July 28, 1926.

9. "John F. Laskey's Service," *WP*, October 21, 1918; "Wan Confesses Killing of Wu, Who Slew Two," *WT*, February 11, 1919; "Secret Grilling Lands Two Chinese in Murder Case, *WH*, February 10, 1919.

10. "Wan Confesses Killing of Wu, Who Slew Two," *WT*, February 11, 1919.

11. "Insists Van Had Nothing to Do With the Killing," *WT*, February 12, 1919.

12. "Wan and Van Held for Grand Jury," *ES*, February 12, 1919.

7. Indictment and Trial

1. *Annual Report of the Commissioners of the District of Columbia*, vol. 1, *Miscellaneous Reports, 1919/1920* (Washington DC: Government Printing Office, 1920), 387–80.

2. *Records of the Columbia Historical Society, Washington DC* (Washington DC: Columbia Historical Society, 1917), 20:86; T. M. Rives, *History of the DC Jail* (unpublished manuscript, 1941); De Benneville Randolph Keim, *Keim's Illustrated Hand-book: Washington and Its Environs* (Washington DC: published by the author, 1888), 208.

3. "Electrocution Must Soon Be Law if Noose Is Not to Take Lives of Five Men in District Jail," *wh*, January 19, 1920; *Annual Report of the Commissioners of the District of Columbia*, vol. 1, *Miscellaneous Reports, 1919/1920* (Washington DC: Government Printing Office, 1920), 375–78.

4. "Murderers' Row Filled; 22 Face Trial or Death," *wh*, August 3, 1919.

5. "Sung Wan, Chinese Held as Slayer, Ill," *wp*, February 13, 1919.

6. "Feminine Voices Interest Chinese," *es*, February 14, 1919.

7. "Wan, Ill, Despondent, May Die in Six Months," *es*, February 15, 1919; "Wan Makes Move for Legal Battle," *es*, February 23, 1919.

8. "Murder Trial Halts," *wp*, September 8, 1919.

9. "Holds Wan Alone Slew Chinese Trio," *es*, September 30, 1919.

10. The Supreme Court of the District of Columbia was renamed the District Court for the District of Columbia by Congress in 1936.

11. "Ziang Sung Wan Pleads Not Guilty of Murder," *es*, October 8, 1919.

12. "Far from Kith and Kin, Lonely Chinese Boy Faces Trial for Triple Killing," *wt*, December 14, 1919.

13. "Quiz 126 in Wan Case," *wp*, December 11, 1919; "Turn Down 100 for Jurors in Wong Killing," *wh*, December 11, 1919; "11 Wan Jurors in Box," *wp*, December 10, 1919; "Far from Kith and Kin, Lonely Chinese Boy Faces Trial for Triple Killing," *wt*, December 14, 1919.

14. "Courthouse to be Preserved in Original Plan," *es*, November 17, 1918.

15. "Wan's Trial Started," *wp*, December 16, 1919.

16. "Clash in Wan Trial," *nyt*, December 17, 1919; "Sharp Questions Put to Kang Li," *es*, December 17, 1919; "Wan Defense Tries to Incriminate Li," *wt*, December 17, 1919.

17. "Wan Induced to Return to Avoid Charge," *es*, December 18, 1919; "Denies Coercion to Get Confession of the Wu Murder," *es*, December 19, 1919; "Sun Wan [*sic*], Held in Triple Crime, Lived Like Lord," *wh*, December 20, 1919.

18. "Wan's Murder Confession Is Heard by Jury," *wh*, December 19, 1919.

19. "Denies Third Degree," *wp*, December 20, 1919.

20. "Sun Wan [*sic*], Held in Triple Crime, Lived Like Lord," *wh*, December 20, 1919.

21. "Denies Wan Was Coerced," *wt*, December 29, 1919.

22. "Quiz Pullman at Wan Trial," *wt*, December 30, 1919.

23. "Pullman Adds Denial of Third Degree on Wan," *wh*, December 31, 1919.

24. "Van Seeks to Save Brother," *wt*, January 5, 1920; "Wan's Confession Is Forced, Is Claim," *es*, January 5, 1920.

25. United States v. Ziang Sung Wan, Testimony of Tsong Ing Van, Supreme Court of the District of Columbia, September 30, 1919; "Van Seeks to Save Brother," *wt*, January 5, 1920; "Wan's Confession Is Forced, Is Claim," *es*, January 5, 1920.

26. "Mysterious Two Named by Van," *wh*, January 6, 1920.

27. "Wan on Stand Denies Crime," *wt*, January 6, 1920.

28. "Oriental Shrewdness of Wan Is Displayed in Cross-Examination," *wt*, January 7, 1920.

29. "Wan Is Found Guilty," *WP*, January 10, 1920.

30. "Van, Brother of Doomed Chinese, to Be Tried For Forgery, States Laskey," *WT*, January 10, 1920.

8. Appeal

1. "Five in Death Cells Set New Record for D.C. Jail; Others Awaiting Trial," *WH*, January 11, 1920; "President Spares Life of C. R. Webster," *WH*, May 18, 1920.

2. "Van, Brother of Doomed Chinese, to Be Tried For Forgery, States Laskey," *WT*, January 10, 1920.

3. "Counsel May Ask New Trial of Wan," *ES*, January 10, 1920; "Guilty Is Verdict of Jury in Case of Chinese Students," *ES*, January 9, 1920; "Wan Jury Out But Half Hour," *WT*, January 9, 1920; "Last Wan Plea Given to Court," *WH*, January 9, 1920.

4. "Will Not Grant Retrial for Wan," *ES*, May 7, 1920; "Wan's Motion for New Trial Denied," *WT*, May 7, 1920.

5. "Wan Faints at Sentence," *WT*, May 14, 1920; "Wan to be Hanged Here December 1," *ES*, May 14, 1920.

6. "President Spares Life of C. R. Webster," *WH*, May 18, 1920.

7. "Wan Appeal Time Extended," *WH*, September 8, 1920; "New Stay Granted to Chinese Slayer," *WT*, November 27, 1920; "Chinaman Again Reprieved," *NYT*, May 27, 1921.

8. "Chinese Slayer, Awaiting Noose, Gains in Weight," *WH*, June 13, 1920; "Autumn Sunshine Filters into Cell on 'Murderers' Row' Where Condemned Men Fret Away Their Last Living Hours," *WT*, October 30, 1921.

9. "Justice Gould Dies Suddenly at Home of Heart Trouble," *ES*, May 20, 1921; "Hanging Postponed," *ES*, May 26, 1921.

10. "Death Penalty in Washington," *WT*, May 23, 1921.

11. "Urge Harding to Save Four from Gallows," *WP*, November 17, 1921.

12. "Harding Won't Commute Death Sentences; Reproves Delegation," *New York Tribune*, November 17, 1921.

13. Letters from James A. Nolan Jr. to Attorney General Harry M. Daugherty, October 4, 1921 and to President Warren G. Harding, October 5, 1921, and from Assistant Attorney General John W. H. Crim to James A. Nolan Jr., October 17, 1921, in General Records of the Department of Justice (RG 60, entry 112, box 3178, file 202765), National Archives and Records Administration, College Park MD.

14. Letters from United States Attorney John E. Laskey to Attorney General Harry M. Daugherty, July 5, 1921, and from United States Attorney Peyton Gordon to Attorney General Harry M. Daugherty, October 21, 1921, in General Records of the Department of Justice (RG 60, entry 112, box 3178, file 202765), National Archives and Records Administration, College Park MD.

15. "Maj. Gordon Takes Oath of Office," *ES*, August 12, 1921.

16. "Forgery Charge Held Up for Hanging Appeal," *WP*, May 2, 1923.

17. Ziang Sung Wan v. United States, Brief for the Appellant, Court of Appeals of District of Columbia, October Term, 1922, 33–34.

18. Bram v. United States, 168 U.S. 532 (1897).

19. The King v. Jane Warickshall, 168 Eng. Rep. 234 (K.B. 1783).

20. Hopt v. Utah, 110 U.S. 574 (1884); "Criminal Law: Evidence: Confessions: Third Degree," *Cornell Law Quarterly* 10, no. 225 (1914–1925): 226; Anne Elizabeth Link, "Fifth Amendment—The Constitutionality of Custodial Confessions," *Journal of Criminal Law and Criminology* 82, no. 4 (Winter 1992): 879; David A. Wollin, "Policing the Police: Should Miranda Violations Bear Fruit?" *Ohio State Law Journal* 53, no. 3 (1992): 814–19.

21. Bram v. United States, 168 U.S. 532 (1897).

22. "Developments in the Law—Confessions," *Harvard Law Review* 79, no. 5 (1966): 960.

23. Bram v. United States, 168 U.S. 532 (1897).

24. For this discussion of the status quo ante that set the stage for the *Wan* decision, I am indebted to Eli Blood-Patterson.

25. Ziang Sung Wan v. United States, Opinion, Court of Appeals of District of Columbia, May 7, 1923.

26. "Death Warrant Issued," *WP*, May 15, 1923; "Chinese Slayer Gets Reprieve of 60 Days," *WP*, May 16, 1923.

9. The Third Degree

1. "Caesar in a Murder Web," *New York World*, April 3, 1895.

2. Welsh S. White, *Miranda's Waning Protections: Police Interrogation Practices after Dickerson* (Ann Arbor: University of Michigan Press, 2001), 14.

3. "Third Degree in Police Parlance," *NYT*, October 6, 1901.

4. "To Abolish the 'Third Degree,'" *NYT*, July 6, 1902.

5. "Police of Buffalo Torture the President's Assailant and Compel the Murderous Anarchist to Confess that He Had Many Accomplices," *San Francisco Call*, September 12, 1901.

6. "The 'Third Degree,'" *New York Tribune*, October 6, 1905.

7. "Our Third Degree Ordeal," *ES*, October 9, 1910.

8. "To Abolish the 'Third Degree,'" *NYT*, July 6, 1902.

9. "The Third Degree," *Baltimore Sun*, February 7, 1907; "U.S. the Only Civilized Nation Where 'Third Degree' Survives," *Spokane Press*, July 26, 1909; "Third Degree Must Go the Latest Dictum," *Pittsburgh Press*, May 7, 1910.

10. "Klein Again Sounds Note of Real Drama," *NYT*, February 2, 1909; "The Play of the Week: 'The Third Degree,'" *NYT*, February 7, 1909; "Audience, After Seeing 'Third Degree' Would Acquit Mrs. Kvalschaug," *Tacoma Times*, December 6, 1909; "Repudiate Their Confessions," *Idaho Statesman*, May 22, 1909.

11. "Chong Saw Leon Kill Sigel Girl," *San Francisco Call*, June 23, 1909; Mary Ting Yi Lui, *The Chinatown Trunk Mystery: Murder, Miscegenation, and Other Dangerous Encounters in Turn-of-the-Century New York City* (Princeton NJ: Princeton University Press, 2007), 201–4.

12. "Torture Still in Use," *NYT*, June 24, 1909.

13. Select Comm. of the U.S. Senate to Investigate the Administration of the Criminal Law by Federal Officials, S. Doc. 62-128, at 1 (First Session, August 4, 1911).

14. "Police Probe Delayed," *ES*, June 13, 1910.

15. Select Comm. of the U.S. Senate to Investigate the Administration of the Criminal Law by Federal Officials, S. Doc. 62-128, at 2–3 (First Session, August 4, 1911).

16. "Congress Is Asked to Probe Arrests in Dynamite Cases," *WT*, April 25, 1911; "Third Degree Committee to Aid Dynamite Cases," *WT*, June 27, 1911; "Wright Must be Impeached, Says Samuel Gompers," *WT*, July 8, 1911; "Gompers Assails Justice Wright," *Richmond Times-Dispatch*, July 9, 1911; "Senator Halts Gompers' Speech," *WH*, July 9, 1911; "Against Kidnapping," *WP*, August 5, 1911.

17. "Hired His Brother to Murder His Paramour," *Spokane Press*, May 11, 1908; "Right Being Made on Montgomery's Saloon," *Spokane Press*, November 12, 1908; "Actions by Pugh Censured," *Spokane Press*, December 24, 1909.

18. "Actions by Pugh Censored," *Spokane Press*, December 24, 1909; "Horrors of the Third Degree Are Exposed by Driskell," *Salt Lake Herald-Republican*, March 23, 1910; "Pardon Board Frees Slayer," *Ogden Standard-Examiner*, April 18, 1920.

19. B. Ogden Chisolm and Hastings H. Hart, *Methods of Obtaining Confessions and Information from Persons Accused of Crime* (New York: Russell Sage Foundation, 1922), 3–6 and 17–18.

10. The Supreme Court

1. "Chinese Loses Move to Escape Gallows," *WP*, May 27, 1923.

2. "Father O'Callaghan Dead; Led Fight to Liberate Wan," *WP*, August 12, 1931; "Rev. P. J. O'Callaghan, Once at Catholic U., Directs Fight," *WP*, February 7, 1926.

3. "Priest Enlists Lawyer to Help Protestant," *The Guardian*, February 27, 1926; "Former Salem School Chieftain Testifies for Chinese Student Charged With Triple Murder," [East Liverpool OH] *Evening Review*, May 4, 1926.

4. Ziang Sung Wan v. United States, Petition for Certiorari to the Court of Appeals of District of Columbia, October Term, 1923, 9–10.

5. Peter G. Renstrom, *The Taft Court: Justices, Rulings, And Legacy* (Santa Barbara CA: ABC-CLIO Supreme Court Handbooks, 2003), 169; Russell W. Galloway, "The Taft Court (1921–29)," *Santa Clara Law Review* 1 (1985): 49; Melvin I. Urofsky, "The Taft Court (1921–1930): Groping for Modernity," in *The United States Supreme Court: The Pursuit of Justice*, ed. Christopher L. Tomlins (New York: Houghton Mifflin, 2005), 216–17; United States v. Lanza, 260 U.S. 377 (1922); Olmstead v. United States, 277 U.S. 438 (1928); Carroll v. United States, 267 U.S. 132 (1925); Hester v. United States, 265 U.S. 57 (1924).

6. Memoranda from Solicitor General James Beck to Attorney William J. Hughes, October 2, 1923 and from U.S. Attorney Peyton Gordon to the Solicitor General, marked to the attention of Attorney William J. Hughes, November 3, 1923, Charles Fahy Papers (MSS 20164), Library of Congress.

7. Memorandum from Solicitor General James Beck to U.S. Attorney Peyton Gordon, December 11, 1923, Charles Fahy Papers (MSS 20164), Library of Congress.

8. Memorandum from U.S. Attorney Peyton Gordon to Solicitor General James Beck, March 1, 1924, Charles Fahy Papers (MSS 20164), Library of Congress.

9. "Chinese Execution Put Off," WP, November 20, 1923; "Delays Hanging of Ziang Sun Wan [*sic*]," ES, March 19, 1924.

10. Letters from William Cullen Dennis to Charles Fahy, May 10, 1924; April 30, 1924; and June 10, 1924, Charles Fahy Papers (MSS 20164), Library of Congress.

11. Letter from William Cullen Dennis to Charles Fahy, May 10, 1924, Charles Fahy Papers (MSS 20164), Library of Congress.

12. Letter from William Cullen Dennis to Charles Fahy, April 30, 1924, and Letter from Ziang Sung Wan to Charles Fahy, May 14, 1924, Charles Fahy Papers (MSS 20164), Library of Congress; "Highest Court Bars Murder Confession Made Under Duress," NYT, October 14, 1924.

13. Letters from Ziang Sung Wan to Charles Fahy, June 10, 1924; June 26, 1924; July 10, 1924; and September 8, 1924; and Letter from Rev. Peter J. O'Callaghan to Charles Fahy, September 11, 1924, Charles Fahy Papers (MSS 20164), Library of Congress; "Hanging Is Postponed," ES, June 24, 1924.

14. Ziang Sung Wan v. United States 266 U.S. 1 (1924), Docket Book of Justice Pierce Butler, October Term, 1923, Office of the Curator, Supreme Court of the United States.

15. Melvin I. Urofsky, *Louis D. Brandeis: A Life* (New York: Pantheon Books, 2009), 473–76.

16. Papers of Louis Dembitz Brandeis, 1881–1966, reel 24, Harvard Law School Library, Cambridge MA.

17. "Lose Fight Against Boy's Confession," WP, October 28, 1920; "New Third Degree Also Invalid, Court of Appeals Holds," WP, November 4, 1924; "Perrygo Escapes Death Sentence," ES, June 8, 1925.

18. "Wins New Trial," WDN, October 14, 1924.

19. "Oyster Will Probe Third Degree," WDN, October 14, 1924; "Two Policemen to Stand Trial on Brutality Charge," WDN, October 20, 1924.

20. "Torture Is Again Condemned," NYT, October 15, 1924.

21. "The Third Degree," *New York Sun*, October 15, 1924.

22. "'Third Degree' Pronounced Criminal," *Pittsburgh Press*, November 11, 1924.

23. "The Police Third Degree," *New York World*, October 31, 1924.

24. Zechariah Chafee Jr., "Compulsory Confessions," *The New Republic 40* (1924): 266–67.

25. "Grilling and the Case of Ziang Sung Wan," WDN, October 14, 1924; "Six Police Face Trial on Assault Charge," WP, November 12, 1924; "Policemen's Cases to be Up Tuesday," WP, October 5, 1924; "Three Montgomery Police Suspended on Charges," WP, October 1, 1924.

26. "Do Washington Police Use the Third Degree?" WDN, October 15, 1924.

27. Letter from Frederic D. McKenney to Charles Fahy, October 23, 1924, Charles Fahy Papers (MSS 20164), Library of Congress.

28. Letter from William Cullen Dennis to Rev. Peter J. O'Callaghan, Charles

Fahy, James A. Nolan, Hugh A. O'Donnell, and Stanley P. Smith, October 13, 1924, Charles Fahy Papers (MSS 20164), Library of Congress; "Execution of Chinese in Killing Postponed," *WP*, October 24, 1924.

11. Retrial

1. "Davis Intervention Saves a Chinese," *BDE*, October 14, 1924; "Highest Court Bars Murder Confession Made Under Duress," *NYT*, October 14, 1924.

2. Excerpts from letters from John William Davis to William Cullen Dennis, September 24, 1923, and to Frederick D. McKenney, January 6, 1924, John William Davis Papers (MS 170), Manuscripts and Archives, Yale University Library.

3. "Highest Court Bars Murder Confession Made Under Duress," *NYT*, October 14, 1924; Letter from William Cullen Dennis to Charles Fahy, October 24, 1924, Charles Fahy Papers (MSS 20164), Library of Congress.

4. Letter from William Cullen Dennis to Charles Fahy, November 1, 1924, Charles Fahy Papers (MSS 20164), Library of Congress.

5. Letter from William Cullen Dennis to Charles Fahy, December 2, 1924, Charles Fahy Papers (MSS 20164), Library of Congress.

6. Letters from William Cullen Dennis to Charles Fahy, November 1, 1924, and to Ziang Sung Wan, November 7, 1924, and from Ziang Sung Wan to James A. O'Shea, November 15, 1924, Charles Fahy Papers (MSS 20164), Library of Congress; "Attorneys Give Up Wan Case," *NYT*, November 25, 1924.

7. Letters from William Cullen Dennis to Charles Fahy, December 2, 1924, and from Hugh A. O'Donnell to Charles Fahy, May 23, 1925, Charles Fahy Papers (MSS 20164), Library of Congress.

8. *Prominent Personages of the Nation's Capital* (Washington DC: Washington Times, 1925), 74–75; "Murdered Chinese Had Property Here," *WP*, May 14, 1919.

9. Letter from Peyton Gordon to Attorney General Harlan F. Stone, November 28, 1924, and Bureau of Investigation Division 2 Memorandum No. 24064 from Mr. Grimes to Director J. Edgar Hoover, December 3, 1924, Headquarters File 62-HQ-9679, Federal Bureau of Investigation, Winchester VA; "Murder Witnesses to Come from China," *ES*, November 30, 1924.

10. "Smiles on His Way to Death," *Rockford Republic*, January 22, 1925; "Twenty-Six Local Police Died Doing Duty," *ES*, October 14, 1926; "District of Columbia Adopts Electric Chair," *Omaha World Herald*, January 30, 1925; "Forty-Five-Year-Old Gallows at Jail Being Dismounted and Burned," *ES*, February 10, 1925; "Trio of Murderers Pay Death Penalty in Electric Chair for Busch Slaying," *ES*, June 22, 1928; Ziang Sung Wan, "Wan: His Own Story," *WT*, July 20, 1926.

11. Letter from United States Attorney Peyton Gordon to Attorney General John G. Sargent, March 7, 1925, General Records of the Department of Justice (RG 60, entry 112, box 3178, file 202765), National Archives and Records Administration, College Park MD.

12. "Stanley Scores D. C. 'Third Degree' in Senate," *WT*, December 13, 1922.

13. "Delay in Wan Execution Puzzles Doctor Kang Li," wh, October 29, 1925; "Wan to Go on Trial in Stafford's Court," wp, November 28, 1925.

14. "Inspector Grant," wp, December 17, 1925; "Selection of Jury May be Completed in Wan Trial Today," wp, January 12, 1926.

15. "Wan Put on Trial Again for Slaying in Chinese Mission," es, January 11, 1926.

16. "Wan Wins Health with Raw Onions and Strong Will," wp, February 28, 1926.

17. "Shorthand Notes of First Wan Trial Found Destroyed," wp, January 15, 1926; "Woman Testifies in Trial of Wan," es, January 18, 1926; "Missing Witness' Evidence Allowed by Wan Trial Judge," es, January 19, 1926.

18. "Surprise Witness Says He Saw Wan at Mission Jan 27," wp, January 21, 1926.

19. "Wan Takes Stand, Tells Life Story," wp, February 5, 1926.

20. "Wan Takes Stand in Own Defense," es, February 4, 1926; "Attempt Made to Link David Lee Wong [*sic*] in Murders," *Binghamton Press*, February 6, 1926.

21. "Attorneys Begin Arguments in Wan Case Before Jury," wp, February 9, 1926.

22. "Wan Jury Fighting 22-Hour Deadlock to Decide His Fate," es, February 10, 1926; "New Trial for Wan Soon, Gordon Says, as Jury Disagrees," wp, February 11, 1926.

23. "Third Trial of Wan is Set for April 5," wp, March 11, 1926.

24. "Gordon Seeks Evidence for Third Wan Trial," wp, April 6, 1926; "Partial Alibi Found for Deceased Chinese Accused of Slayings," *Binghamton Press*, April 16, 1926.

25. "Chinese Goes on Trial for Third Time for Killing," *Binghamton Press*, March 31, 1936; "Wan Jury is Obtained After 600 Are Passed," wp, April 20, 1926; "Third Wan Murder Trial Opened With Selection of Jury," wp, April 13, 1926; "250 More Called for Murder Jury," wp, April 16, 1926.

26. "Murder Story Is Told As Wan Trial Starts," wp, April 21, 1926.

27. "Burlingame Admits Modifying Previous Testimony on Wan," wp, April 24, 1926; "Wan Prosecutors Took Lee on Parties," wp, April 27, 1926; "Police Detective's Version of Murder Given at Wan Trial," wp, April 28, 1926.

28. "Wan Case Witness Favors Defendant," wp, April 22, 1926.

29. "Wan Counsel Seek to Smash Evidence Against Defendant," wp, April 30, 1926.

30. "State's Releasing of Watches Stirs Counsel for Wan," wp, May 4, 1926; "Porter Says Wan in Station at Time of Check Incident," wp, May 6, 1926.

31. "Jury Will Be Given Wan Murder Case for Verdict Today," wp, May 12, 1926.

32. "Murder Case Jury Reported As 11–1 to Acquit Chinese," wp, May 13, 1926.

33. "Jury is Dismissed in Third Wan Trial," wp, May 14, 1926; "Motion to Dismiss Wan Murder Case to Be Made Today," wp, May 27, 1926.

34. "Wan Will Be Tried Again in Oct. or Set Free Soon," wp, May 28, 1926.

35. "Ziang Zun [*sic*] Wan, Chinese Thrice Tried for Murder, Long in Prison, to be Freed," bde, June 5, 1926; Frederic William Wile, "Washington," *Poughkeepsie Eagle-News*, June 21, 1926.

36. "Chinese Wins Freedom After 7 Years in Gallows' Shadow: To Return to Blind Mother," bde, June 27, 1926; "Wan Wins Fight For Liberty," es, June 16, 1926.

37. "Wan Wins Fight For Liberty," es, June 16, 1926.

12. Freedom

1. "Wan Case Likely to Start Inquiry," *ES*, June 17, 1926.

2. "Trial of Chinese Stirs Law Reform," *NYT*, July 25, 1926.

3. "The Model Criminal Code," *Springfield Republican*, May 13, 1930; "Committee on American Law Institute," *Chicago Bar Association Record* 90, no. 5 (Chicago: Chicago Bar Association, 1926), 2; "Over a Million Serious Crimes the Yearly Toll," *Lincoln Evening Journal*, December 13, 1934.

4. Michael Palmiotto and Prabha Unnithan, *Policing and Society: A Global Approach* (Clifton Park NY: Delmar, 2011), 99; "Crime Commissions—More Recent Commissions, The Political Context Of The Crime Commissions, Bibliography," American Law and Legal Information website, accessed December 1, 2015, http://law.jrank.org/pages/828/Crime-Commissions.html.

5. Ziang Sung Wan, "Wan's Own Story of Fight for Life," *WT*, July 22, 1926; Ziang Sung Wan, "Wan: His Own Story," *WT*, July 26, 1926.

6. Ziang Sung Wan, "Wan: His Own Story," *WT*, July 20, 1926; Ziang Sung Wan, "Wan Shows How the Check Stub Was Signed by Another," *WT*, July 22, 1926; Ziang Sung Wan, "Wan: His Own Story," *WT*, July 23, 1926.

7. Ziang Sung Wan, "Wan: His Own Story," *WT*, July 23 and 26, 1926.

8. Letter from William Cullen Dennis to Charles Fahy, October 24, 1927, Charles Fahy Papers (MSS 20164), Library of Congress.

9. "Chinese Boy Here Recuperating from Tragic Experience," *Warren* [PA] *Tribune*, October 29, 1926; "Accused of Three Murders, Behind Bars for Seven Years, Now a Useful Citizen," *Greensboro Daily Record*, June 3, 1927.

10. Huang Qiaoqi (黄乔奇), *Huang Zuoting Yu Gengkuan Liu Mei Xuesheng* (黄佐庭与庚款留美学生), Sina website, accessed December 1, 2015, http://blog.sina.com.cn/s/blog_74ca0b6d0101ansz.html.

13. The Wickersham Report

1. Inaugural Address of Herbert Hoover, March 4, 1929, Herbert Hoover Presidential Library website, accessed November 25, 2015, http://www.hoover.archives.gov/info/inauguralspeech.html; Samuel Walker, "The Engineer as Progressive: The Wickersham Commission in the Arc of Herbert Hoover's Life and Work," *Marquette Law Review* 96, no. 4 (Summer 2013): 1165–76.

2. "Wickersham Dies in a Taxicab at 77," *NYT*, January 26, 1936.

3. "History of the Commission's Activities Since its Appointment in May, 1929," *NYT*, January 21, 1931.

4. "Crime Commission Will Divide Tasks," *WP*, May 31, 1929; "Wickersham Gives Commission Plans," *NYT* May 31, 1929.

5. Franklin E. Zimring, "The Accidental Crime Commission: Its Legacies and Lessons, Barrock Lecture, Wickersham Commission Symposium," *Marquette Law Review* 96, no. 4 (Summer 2013): 996–98; "Wickersham Slate Finally Is Cleared," *NYT* August 24, 1931.

6. Franklin E. Zimring, "The Accidental Crime Commission: Its Legacies and

Lessons, Barrock Lecture, Wickersham Commission Symposium," *Marquette Law Review* 96, no. 4 (Summer 2013): 1000–1007; Peter Lee, "When America Said No!" *Counterpunch* 16, no. 13 (July 1–31, 2009): 1.

7. Peter Lee, "Keeping Up With the Wickershams," July 28, 2009, China Matters website, accessed July 8, 2015, http://chinamatters.blogspot.com/2009/07/keeping -up-with-wickershams.html.

8. Peter Lee, "When America Said No!" *Counterpunch* 16, no. 13 (July 1–31, 2009): 1; Welsh S. White, *Miranda's Waning Protections: Police Interrogation Practices after Dickerson* (Ann Arbor: University of Michigan Press, 2001), 17.

9. "W. H. Pollak Dies; Leader at Bar, 53," *NYT*, October 3, 1940; "Carl S. Stern, Lawyer in Noted Cases, Dies at 86," *NYT*, December 28, 1970.

10. Zechariah Chafee Jr., "Compulsory Confessions" *The New Republic* 40 (1924): 266–67.

11. National Commission on Law Observance and Enforcement, *Lawlessness in Law Enforcement* (Washington DC: U.S. Government Printing Office, 1931), 3–6 and 19.

12. National Commission on Law Observance and Enforcement, *Lawlessness in Law Enforcement* (Washington DC: U.S. Government Printing Office, 1931), 21–24.

13. National Commission on Law Observance and Enforcement, *Lawlessness in Law Enforcement* (Washington DC: U.S. Government Printing Office, 1931), 24–31.

14. National Commission on Law Observance and Enforcement, *Lawlessness in Law Enforcement* (Washington DC: U.S. Government Printing Office, 1931), 63, 72, and 253–54.

15. National Commission on Law Observance and Enforcement, *Lawlessness in Law Enforcement* (Washington DC: U.S. Government Printing Office, 1931), 56–57, 66–67, 158–59, and 239.

16. National Commission on Law Observance and Enforcement, *Lawlessness in Law Enforcement* (Washington DC: U.S. Government Printing Office, 1931), 73–75.

17. National Commission on Law Observance and Enforcement, *Lawlessness in Law Enforcement* (Washington DC: U.S. Government Printing Office, 1931), 181–90.

18. National Commission on Law Observance and Enforcement, *Lawlessness in Law Enforcement* (Washington DC: U.S. Government Printing Office, 1931), 191.

19. "Police Methods," *Dallas Morning News*, August 12, 1931; "Better Look Into It," *Cleveland Plain Dealer*, August 11, 1931.

20. "Let There Be No Snap Judgment on Wickersham Report Police Charges," *San Francisco Chronicle*, August 12, 1931; "'Third Degree' Exposure," *Greensboro Daily News*, August 12, 1931; "Police and 'Third Degree,'" *Trenton Evening Times*, August 15, 1931.

21. Zechariah Chafee Jr., *Blessings of Liberty* (New York: Lippincott, 1956), 292; "Against Third Degree," *Springfield Republican*, August 11, 1931; G. Daniel Lassiter, ed., *Interrogations, Confessions, and Entrapment* (New York: Springer Science and Business Media, 2004), 55.

22. "Law Body Hits Brutal Third Degrees," *WP*, August 11, 1931; "Police Deny Wan Was Ill-Treated," *WP*, August 11, 1931; "Wan Third Degree Charges Disputed," *ES*, August 10, 1931.

23. G. Daniel Lassiter, ed., *Interrogations, Confessions, and Entrapment* (New York: Springer Science and Business Media, 2004), 55–56; Welsh S. White, *Miranda's Waning Protections: Police Interrogation Practices after Dickerson* (Ann Arbor: University of Michigan Press, 2001), 21.

24. It was Worth R. Kidd, *Police Interrogation* (New York: R. V. Basuino, 1940).

14. The Road to Miranda

1. Powell v. Alabama, 287 U.S. 45 (1932).

2. Brown v. Mississippi, 297 U.S. 278, (1936).

3. "Developments in the Law—Confessions," *Harvard Law Review* 79, no. 5 (1966): 962.

4. Anne Elizabeth Link, "Fifth Amendment—The Constitutionality of Custodial Confessions," *Journal of Criminal Law and Criminology* 82, no. 4 (1992): 878–903; Charles J. Ogletree, "Are Confessions Really Good for the Soul?: A Proposal to Mirandize 'Miranda,'" *Harvard Law Review* 100, no. 7 (May, 1987): 1826–45.

5. Ashcraft v. Tennessee, 322 U.S. 143 (1944). See also Yale Kamisar's 2011 speech, "The Rise, Fall and Decline of Miranda," October 18, 2011, University of Washington School of Law website, accessed January 28, 2016, http://www.law.washington .edu/multimedia/2011/YaleKamisar/Transcript.aspx.

6. Haynes v. Washington, 373 U.S. 503 (1963); Culombe v. Connecticut, 367 U.S. 568 (1961).

7. Culombe v. Connecticut, 367 U.S. 568 (1961).

8. Malloy v. Hogan, 378 U.S. 1 (1964).

9. For in-depth discussions of the evolution of tests for the admission of custodial confessions, see Anne Elizabeth Link, "Fifth Amendment—The Constitutionality of Custodial Confessions" *Journal of Criminal Law and Criminology* 82, no. 4 (1992): 878–903; Charles J. Ogletree, "Are Confessions Really Good for the Soul? A Proposal to Mirandize 'Miranda,'" *Harvard Law Review* 100, no. 7 (May 1987): 1826–45; Yale Kamisar, "A Dissent from the Miranda Dissents: Some Comments on the 'New' Fifth Amendment and the Old 'Voluntariness' Test," *Michigan Law Review* 65 (1966): 59–104; David A. Wollin, "Policing the Police: Should Miranda Violations Bear Fruit?" *Ohio State Law Journal* 53, no. 3 (1992): 812–19.

10. Miranda v. Arizona, 384 U.S. 436 (1966).

11. Miranda v. Arizona, 384 U.S. 436 (1966).

Epilogue

1. "False Confessions More Prevalent Among Teens," September 9, 2013, Innocence Project website, accessed April 25, 2016, http://www.innocenceproject.org /false-confessions-more-prevalent-among-teens; Samuel L. Gross and Michael Shaffer, "Exonerations in the United States, 1989–2012," Report by the National Registry of Exonerations, June 2012.

2. "Mrs. Blalock's Charges Bring Row at Inquiry," *WP*, January 30, 1929; "Goes

Back in Command of the Second Precinct Early Today," *WP*, March 13, 1929; "Grand Jury Clears Capt. Burlingame," *WP*, April 2, 1929.

3. "Zechariah Chafee, Jr. 72, Dead: Lawyer, Civil Liberties Champion," *NYT*, February 9, 1957.

4. "Solicitor General: Charles Fahy," United States Department of Justice website, accessed December 1, 2015, http://www.justice.gov/osg/bio/charles-fahy.

5. "Ex-D.C. Judge Peyton Gordon is Dead at 76," *WP*, September 18, 1946.

6. "Grant Obsequies To Be Tomorrow; Rites by Masons," *WP*, December 17, 1925; "Throngs of Varied Mourners Attend Funeral of Grant," *WP*, December 19, 1925.

7. "George D. Horning, Jr. Dies, *AU* Emeritus Law Professor," *WP*, February 12, 1974.

8. "Col. Edward J. Kelly, 62, Dies at Dinner 20 Days After Retiring," *ES*, February 21, 1946.

9. "Wilton J. Lambert, Attorney, 63, Dead," *NYT*, July 23, 1935; John Clagett Proctor, *Washington, Past and Present: A History* (New York: Lewis Historical Publishing, 1930–1932), 485–86.

10. "John E. Laskey, 1868–1945," *Records of the Columbia Historical Society, Washington, DC* (Washington: Historical Society of Washington DC, 1944/1945), 421–22.

11. "Delay in Wan Execution Puzzles Doctor Kang Li," *WH*, October 29, 1925; York Lo (羅元旭), *Dong Cheng Xi Jiu: Qige Huaren Jidujiao Jiazu Yu Zhongxi Jiaoliu Bainian* (東成西就—七個華人基督教家族與中西交流百年) (Hong Kong: Joint Publishing, 2012), 41.

12. "Frederic McKenney, Long-Time Attorney Here, Dies at 86," *ES*, June 27, 1949; "Frederic D. McKenney," *ES*, June 29, 1949.

13. "Father O'Callaghan, Abstinence League President, Is Dead," *Chicago Tribune*, August 12, 1931.

14. "Hugh A. O'Donnell, Ex-Times Aide, Dies," *NYT*, August 24, 1941; "300 Attend Rites for H. A. O'Donnell," *NYT*, August 25, 1941.

15. "James O'Shea, Criminal Lawyer Here for 40 Years, Dies at 71," *WP*, December 29, 1949.

16. "Pullman Rites Today," *WP*, February 24, 1920.

17. Chinese Exclusion Act Case File for Tsong Iung Wan (a.k.a. Tsung Iung Van), Record Group 85, Records of the Immigration and Naturalization Service, File 12017/50930, National Archives and Records Administration, San Bruno California; Certificate of Incorporation, Chinese League of America, Inc., January 11, 1950, New York State Department of State, Division of Corporations; "Chinese League Formed," *NYT*, January 22, 1950.

18. "Wickersham Dies in a Taxicab at 77," *NYT*, January 26, 1936.

SELECTED BIBLIOGRAPHY

Archival Collections

Federal Bureau of Investigation
  FBI Headquarters file 62-HQ-9679, *Ziang Sung Wan v. United States*, Records Management Division, Winchester VA.
Harvard University
  Louis Dembitz Brandeis Papers, Harvard Law School Library. *Wan v. United States*, October term, 1923, box 26-2, and October term, 1924, boxes 30-9 to 30-12.
Library of Congress
  Charles Fahy Papers, correspondence, boxes 98 and 99, Manuscript Division, Washington DC.
  William Howard Taft Papers, William Howard Taft–Helen Herron Taft Correspondence, 1882–1929, reel 28, letter of April 8, 1924.
National Archives, College Park MD
  Record group 60, General Records of the Department of Justice, *Ziang Sung Wan v. United States*, entry 112, box 3178, file 202765.
National Archives, San Bruno CA
  Case files of Chinese immigrants, record group 85, Ziang Sun Wan, file 27784/1, and Tsong Iung Wan (a.k.a. Tsung Iung Van), file 12017/50930.
National Archives, Washington DC
  Record group 21, records of the District Courts of the United States, District of Columbia, criminal case file 35614, *United States v. Ziang Sung Wan*, box 295.
  Record group 21, records of the District Courts of the United States, District of Columbia, criminal case file 35614, *United States v. Tsong Ing Van*, box 295.
  Record group 267, records of the United States Supreme Court, appellate case 29761, *Ziang Sung Wan v. United States*, box 7383.
  Record group 276, records of the United States Court of Appeals, District of Columbia Circuit, general docket, case 3807, *Ziang Sung Wan v. United States*, official trial transcripts, box 335; briefs, box 366; clerk's files, box 83, and opinions, box 68.
Supreme Court of the United States
  Office of the Curator. Docket book of Justice Pierce Butler, October term, 1923, page 278.

University of Virginia

> *University of Virginia Catalogues*, 1890–1900, call number LD5667, Albert and Shirley Small Special Collections Library, Charlottesville VA.

Yale University

> John William Davis Papers (MS 170). Series VII, Law Practice, box 162, *Ziang Sung Wan v. United States* 266 U.S. 1 (1924). Manuscripts and Archives, Yale University Library.

Published Works

Burlingame, Guy E. "Three Murders That Shocked Washington." *Master Detective*, April, May, June, and July 1931.

Chafee, Zechariah, Jr. "Compulsory Confessions." *The New Republic* 40 (1924): 266–67.

"Developments in the Law—Confessions." *Harvard Law Review* 79, no. 5 (1966): 935–1119.

"Extending Miranda to Administrative Investigations." *Virginia Law Review* 56, no. 4 (May 1970): 690–715.

Godsey, Mark A. "Rethinking the Involuntary Confession Rule: Toward a Workable Test for Identifying Compelled Self-Incrimination." *California Law Review* 93, no. 2 (2005): 465–540.

Harbaugh, William Henry. *Lawyer's Lawyer: The Life of John W. Davis*. Charlottesville: University of Virginia Press, 1990.

Kamisar, Yale. "A Dissent from the Miranda Dissents: Some Comments on the 'New' Fifth Amendment and the Old 'Voluntariness' Test." *Michigan Law Review* 65 (1966): 59–104.

Link, Anne Elizabeth. "Fifth Amendment—The Constitutionality of Custodial Confessions." *Journal of Criminal Law and Criminology* 82, no. 4 (1992): 878–903.

Mason, Alpheus Thomas. *The Supreme Court from Taft to Burger*. Baton Rouge: Louisiana State University Press, 1979.

McKenney, Frederic D. *Ziang Sung Wan v. United States, U.S. Supreme Court Transcript of Record with Supporting Pleadings*. Gale Ecco, U.S. Supreme Court Records, 2011.

National Commission on Law Observance and Enforcement. *Lawlessness in Law Enforcement*. Washington DC: U.S. Government Printing Office, 1931.

Ogletree, Charles J. "Are Confessions Really Good for the Soul? A Proposal to Mirandize 'Miranda.'" *Harvard Law Review* 100, no. 7 (May 1987): 1826–45.

Penney, Steven. "Theories of Confession Admissibility: A Historical View." *American Journal of Criminal Law* 25 (Spring 1998): 309–82.

Post, Robert. "Federalism, Positivism, and the Emergence of the American Administrative State: Prohibition in the Taft Court Era." *William and Mary Law Review* 48, no. 1 (2006).

Stokes, H. N., ed. "Ziang Sung Wan." *The O. E. Literary Critic* 15, no. 22 (1926).

Strum, Philippa. *Louis D. Brandeis: Justice for the People*. Cambridge MA: Harvard University Press, 1984.

Thomas, George C., and Richard A. Leo. *Confessions of Guilt: From Torture to Miranda and Beyond.* New York: Oxford University Press, 2012.

Tomkovicz, James J. *Constitutional Exclusion: The Rules, Rights, and Remedies that Strike the Balance between Freedom and Order.* New York: Oxford University Press, 2011.

Urofsky, Melvin I. *Louis D. Brandeis: A Life.* New York: Pantheon, 2009.

Walker, Samuel. *Popular Justice: A History of American Criminal Justice.* New York: Oxford University Press, 1980.

White, Welsh S. *Miranda's Waning Protections: Police Interrogation Practices after Dickerson.* Ann Arbor: University of Michigan Press, 2001.

Wollin, David A. "Policing the Police: Should Miranda Violations Bear Fruit?" *Ohio State Law Journal* 53, no. 3 (1992): 805–68.

INDEX

Page numbers in italic indicate illustrations.